INTEGRATING PSYCHOLOGY AND SPIRITUALITY?

INTEGRATING PSYCHOLOGY AND SPIRITUALITY?

Richard L. Gorsuch

Westport, Connecticut
London

Library of Congress Cataloging-in-Publication Data

Gorsuch, Richard L.
  Integrating psychology and spirituality? / Richard L. Gorsuch.
    p.   cm.
  Includes bibliographical references and index.
  ISBN 0–275–97372–7 (alk. paper)
  1. Psychology and religion.   I. Title.
  BF51.G66   2002
  291.1'75—dc21   2002021573

British Library Cataloguing in Publication Data is available.

Library of Congress Catalog Card Number: 2002021573
ISBN: 0–275–97372–7

First published in 2002

Praeger Publishers, 88 Post Road West, Westport, CT 06881
An imprint of Greenwood Publishing Group, Inc.
www.praeger.com

Printed in the United States of America

The paper used in this book complies with the
Permanent Paper Standard issued by the National
Information Standards Organization (Z39.48–1984).

10 9 8 7 6 5 4 3 2 1

To
Jacob
Andrew
Ethen
Samantha

Contents

Exhibits

Acknowledgments

Many people have aided the development of this book by critiquing drafts. Among those providing chapter-by-chapter feedback are Heather Brikett Catleu, Al Dueck, Ralph Hood, Tim Gener, Larry Erlbaum, Elizabeth Maynard, Lamar Robert, and Don Walker. The critiques of students in classes at Loma Linda University and Fuller Theological Seminary and the several secretaries who have worked on parts of this project are also gratefully acknowledged. Each critiqued the work from his or her own perspective, and that distinctiveness of perspective was most helpful in understanding the variety of ways the arguments could be viewed. A special word of thanks goes to Nancey Murphy; while she did not read a draft of this book, she did provide me with an introduction to postmodernism that encouraged me to crystallize my ideas in the area of integration. Of course, I adapted the critiques to my own purposes and so can blame no one except myself for any errors.

How to Read This Book

This book differs in style from both textbooks and research articles with which the reader may be familiar in the sense that it is designed to be both a discussion of [several disciplines] and the reflections of the author. As you read the book, it may be helpful for you to conceptualize it this way, reflecting yourself on the ways in which you integrate your scholarly or professional pursuits with one another and with your personal interests and experiences.

Elizabeth Maynard
(from an e-mail on an early draft, 8 January 1999)

PART I

THE NATURE OF
INTEGRATION

CHAPTER 1

What Is Integration of Disciplines?

"Psychology can show that religion is just silly superstition."

"We Christians [Moslems] have the Bible [Koran]—we don't need psychology."

"Psychology can sift out the universal truths that all religions share from the myths of primitive peoples."

"Until our religious leaders learn sufficient psychology, we will lose the next generation."

"A Christian clinical psychologist? Impossible."

These are among the statements one might hear about relating psychology and spirituality. But are any such statements reasoned positions based on clear definitions and assumptions? Do they relate to modern psychology and modern spirituality? What are the implications for applied psychology, ethics, and everyday life? Exploring such questions is what this project is about. We shall range broadly, starting with more basic issues in Chapters 1 and 2 (including the definition of integration and the "truth" of psychology and spirituality). In Chapters 3 and 4 we explore what psychology may say to spirituality, and what spirituality may say to psychology. Then we combine both psychology and spirituality in examining applied clinical and social psychological issues in the last two chapters.

From thoughtfully reading this book, you can expect to understand the bases for integrating psychology and spirituality. The book includes integrative discussions around several issues. These discussions will serve as examples for your own integration. Hopefully, this project will stimulate more serious dialogue between the several disciplines concerned with psychology and spirituality, and also provide integration training for professionals such as clinical psychologists and ministers.

I will warn you that, in some places, I am speaking "tongue in cheek." I do hope that you will occasionally chuckle at some examples or wordings that I have used, for I do so in writing. That does not mean that the examples or statements are wrong or to be ignored, but it does mean that we should never take ourselves too seriously, for we are humans with all the fallibility inherent thereto.

BEGINNING DEFINITIONS

To address integrating psychology and spirituality, the first task of this project is to establish the meanings of terms or, at least, the definitions as used here. Here is the first definition:

> **Disciplinary integration is when two or more disciplines are jointly brought to bear on the same issue so that decisions about that issue reflect the contributions of both disciplines. The issue may be about how one discipline carries out its work or may be a problem that more than one discipline work together to solve.**

Here are some brief illustrations involving integration across disciplines. To help develop rural agriculture among the hill peoples of Thailand, the developmental team must bring together (i.e., integrate) the expertise of both agriculture and cross-cultural studies. The former provides information on what crops to try and the latter provides information on what crops will be acceptable to the culture. While relying on only one of the two disciplines may be helpful, the chances of success are greatly improved by involving both. The present project uses this definition of integration to consider the integration of psychology and spirituality.

The practice of law is also the practice of ethics. Shytov (Personal communication, 2000) considers the obligations of law from a joint framework of psychology and spirituality; the psychology of Leon Petrazycki and the spirituality of Thomas Aquinas. The issue under discussion is how a judge may apply the law as Christian law. Examples are drawn from actual cases from the courts of four different countries.

Professionals translating and understanding old documents, such as editions of the Buddhist or Christian scriptures, need to know which of several editions is oldest. Experts in methods of determining age by the type of ink used, for example, are able to tell us whether it is possible to decide if one document is thirty years older than another or if it is only possible to decide if one document is three-hundred years older than another. Integrating the knowledge from two areas of study is required to understand the relationships among the documents.

Integration is a task and a goal. We *integrate* rural agriculture and cross-cultural studies to increase crop production among the hill tribes. *Integration* has been achieved when a decision has been made about the relative age of the manuscripts. It is specific to a situation, as in these examples.

Throughout the book there are occasional exercises that you may find of interest. Because they are generally to prepare you for what follows, please complete each exercise at the point it occurs before reading further. Who knows? An occasional exercise may expand your integration. If you are totally lost as to what integration is, that's OK. This book will help you develop some possibilities. In this case, you may wish to postpone an exercise until you have read more.

EXERCISE

1. Take out a sheet of paper.
2. On the top half of the sheet, write an example of what you feel is excellent integration. Be as concrete as possible.
3. On the bottom half of the sheet, write an example of what you feel is an obviously failed attempt at integration. Be as concrete as possible.
4. Consider briefly the differences between your two statements. Use this as background to help understand what is meant by integration in this book.

Of course, no two scholars agree on the exact boundaries of this topic so it not a question of your trying to guess what I shall say. Nevertheless, this exercise will provide a starting point for your understanding of what is meant in this book by the term.

Psychology is the scientific study of human behavior in its immediate context. This definition has several essential elements. First, and this is probably no surprise, we are concerned with "scientific study." In fact, many discussions in this book are about science and spirituality because they apply to all sciences, not just psychology. To lay the foundation for integration with psychology, the broader issues of integrating with science is considered first; whenever the term "science" is used, it explicitly includes psychology. Second, we are concerned here with "human behavior." Others define psychology to include non–human data. I have no problem with that, and might use that definition in another context. However, the task of integration is a distinctly human task, and so we are restricting our psychology accordingly. Third, perhaps the most unique part of this definition is that we're defining psychology as studying people in their "immediate context." This is necessary because sociology has a number of research and theoretical programs that are similar to but also distinct from our approach here. From my observation of psychologists, practically all our work involves people interacting with that which is in their immediate surroundings. We psychologists only consider, for example, norms that are communicated to the individual by vocal, written, or other direct procedures. This differentiates psychology from sociology, which includes the study of culture and is more concerned with the broader context that produces or influences the immediate environment. Of course, there are border areas in which both psychologists and sociologists work.

Spirituality is the quest for understanding ourselves in relationship to our view of ultimate reality, and to live in accordance with that understanding. This is a broad definition, and many readers will have their own definition from within their spiritual tradition (even as I do, which is noted later). These definitions will almost always be a special case of this definition based upon ultimate reality as the definer has found it.

The breath of possibilities for spirituality includes the major religious traditions—we Christians base it in God and Jesus—but spirituality as a term is not limited to religious traditions. "Ultimate reality" may or may not have a mystical side or an organizational side to it; that depends on what form spirituality takes for a particular person. Nor is spirituality linked to any one approach or to any one discipline. The disciplines traditionally most related to spirituality include philosophy and theology, but not all parts of those disciplines are concerned with spirituality. When spirituality is used in this book, it includes the relevant areas of philosophy, theology, ethics, and comparative religions.

Spirituality consists of our relationship to the broader reality of which we are a part, our role in this reality, and how we align ourselves, including our behavior, to be consistent with that reality. Religions, worldviews, and philosophical systems such as Beyondism (explained later) are generally examples of this, provided that they are integrated with one's life. While for this project spirituality includes mysticisms, it is not limited to them. While for people of a traditional faith spirituality is almost the same as religion (Zinnbower et al., 1997; Spilka & McIntosh, personal communication, 1997), spirituality includes religious faiths but is not limited to them. While I use my spiritual base—Christianity—as the example of spirituality in this project, spirituality is not limited to it.

Ethics is for some the essence of spirituality and for others an essential aspect of it. It involves the integration of multiple areas, with the spiritual areas concerned about the broader reality and goals and the social science areas providing any relevant information that is available from them. The interactions are—as is generally true of integration—complex and varied. (While Murphy, 1997, argues for ethics becoming a separate science, the tasks she projects for it are mostly psychological in nature and often have considerable psychological work already done on them; see Gorsuch & Malony, 1976, Chapter 9). For this project, ethics is seen as a part of spirituality. Ethics, then, is one area of integration between spirituality and social science. Given how I define spirituality, ethics is an essential part of it for all and may be the primary content for some who are less religiously or mystically oriented.

In terms of academic areas, spirituality is studied through several disciplines, including philosophy. **Philosophy's task is to provide coherent explanations to questions transcending any particular discipline or type of experience** (based on Clayton, 1989, p. 104). Any definition of philosophy is problematic, for the definitions of philosophy used by various thinkers in this century have varied widely. This definition does include questions that could be labeled metaphysical and also includes ethics, although others may treat ethics independently.

Theology is the study of God, ultimate reality, or religion, including the relationship with people and the ethics resulting therefrom. This definition is not uncommon, but there are some special interpretations. The first is the problem of people who are spiritual, or who have a religion, but have no explicit supernatural deity. Those are included within our phrase "philosophy and theology," and you may consider them part of either philosophy or theology. Of special interest in the definition is "the ethics resulting therefrom." Theology, as defined here, is not abstracted from life itself but is always, at some point, concerned with what we do with our lives.

The emphasis on ethics in the definition of theology does overlap philosophical ethics. In fact, I toyed with using "theology–philosophy" in place of theology alone but decided that would be too awkward for general use. There will be cases where I use the terms philosophy and theology interchangeably or use "theology–philosophy" to remind us that both may be involved. Whenever theology or philosophy is involved, spirituality may also be involved.

There are many forms of theology, including the world religions. Christianity as one theology is, of course, based in a Christocentric system. I will use the term "Christianity" often, and it should be understood in the light of classical Biblical-based and Christ-centered theology integrated into experience. Thus, **Christianity is the explicit and implicit application of New Testament theology to life**. The "explicit and implicit" phrase is included because Christianity may be lived and lived well without formal, explicit theological thinking. Being New Testament–oriented means it is inherently Christ centered. Also note that "New Testament theology" includes the Old Testament as interpreted through the New Testament paradigm. Some traditions, such as Roman Catholic and Orthodox, add the Church's theology.

So spirituality can be approached from several disciplines, including philosophy, ethics, and Christian and non-Christian theologies. All these are within the humanities, and so all references to the humanities explicitly include disciplines concerned with spirituality.

Each of the areas—psychology, philosophy, and theology and Christianity—is the same in some respects. All are concerned with explanations of how or why questions, and all occur in most societies. For example, tribal legends often integrate theology, philosophy, and psychology in answer to how or why questions. The disciplines do differ in which area explanations are sought and how the explanations are justified. For example, all sciences are interested in justifying their explanations by scientific research. Classically, philosophy has justified explanations by the reasonableness and coherence of the rationales. Theology justifies itself in terms of its relationships to Biblical understanding. All are concerned with explanations and the justification thereof (Clayton, 1989).

Note the importance of the disciplines. In this book I assume that we are influenced by our personal beliefs and values in our professional lives as well as our personal lives. This point is so basic to the project that it is not debated. In that sense, everyone is involved in integration all the time. But are they "doing integration"? By many definitions, yes. By the definitions in this project, no.

The type of integration considered here only occurs when the disciplines of psychology and the relevant spirituality are engaged. In addition, accidental and unexamined integration happens continuously. A classical distinction is between more unconscious or unexamined assumptions and commitments of a culture and more thoughtfully examined assumptions and commitments within a culture. The first, referred to by the German *Weltbild*, or "world picture," consists of a common outlook, generally unconscious and quite stable. The latter are referred to as *Weltanschauungen* or "worldviews," which are basic conscious convictions not susceptible to scientific investigation, and there may be several in the same culture. Note that while world picture (*Weltbild*) is singular because each is the set of the unconscious assumptions of all within a culture, worldviews (*Weltanschauungen*) is plural because there are generally several within a culture (Marshall, Griffioen, & Mouw, 1989; Griffioen, 1989). While plural, the latter are rational in the sense that they can be examined and compared for relative merit. This project is to encourage deliberate, thoughtful integration that is informed by the relevant disciplines to assist in developing worldviews.

Hoshmand (1998) has edited an interesting book with chapters by senior psychologists who reflect on their careers, profession, and the values behind the choices they made. Is this integration? Mostly the chapters are post hoc descriptions of professional decisions in the context of their personal values. This is not, however, complete integration in the sense of bringing together two disciplines. Integration requires involvement of the methods and conclusions of each of the disciplines, and thus only begins with personal stories.

Must one have formal education in both disciplines? I'm sure that many readers will wish I were more informed in some area, namely the ones in which they have expertise! However, this project is an introduction because it only assumes the reader is educated at the liberal arts level. More important, it assumes the willingness to think integratively with the motivation to pursue that task wherever it may take us. Hopefully it will stimulate more serious dialogue between experts in several disciplines, and thus further integration.

The definitions here suggest that integrative dialogue between psychology and spirituality is possible. Hopefully when you finish reading this book you will have seen and achieved some integration yourself. As Jones (1994) suggests, not only is the dialogue possible, there is much to favor it and the intrinsic overlap between the areas strongly suggests it is useful.

CLASSICAL MODELS OF INTEGRATION

Niebuhr (1956) laid out a format for relating Christianity and culture that shows various possible models for integration between any spirituality and another discipline. These can be generalized to extended from "religion against culture" to "religion of culture" to "Christ and culture in paradox" to "religion and culture in dialogue." The first possibility is a complete domination of one's thinking by religion so that it determines the culture. Any religious group that follows this model insists that the laws of their religion become the laws of their culture, such as the Islamic movements for countries to base their laws solely on the Koran. Indeed, from this perspective culture and science are rewritten, as much as politically possible, to be explicitly tied to that religion. If our integration model were the first of Niebuhr's, religion against culture, that would mean that we would rewrite psychology and philosophy so that it would be solely religion based. The second case, religion of culture, means that integration takes place by rewriting religion in the most compatible manner possible with a given culture. In either case, integration becomes primarily the translating of terms from culture (i.e., philosophy and psychology) to theology or vice versa.

The more extreme "creation science" is received by scientists as a case of theology over science. This position notes that the Bible tells in Genesis that the world was made in just seven days and interprets this to mean seven of our twenty-four-hour days. In addition, the rest of the Bible is seen as indicating that the world has existed only a relatively short time, and so science must be rewritten to these conclusions. For example, they argue that strata in geological formations show nothing about the history of the Earth; all the fossils and indications of old age were just created in the strata. Creation science also holds there was a worldwide flood, and the lack of sufficient water to flood all the Earth at one time is worked into the revisions of science. This narrow "creation science"—and there are other creationist positions compatible with science—can be challenged as to whether it is science at all (Friedlander, 1995).

Often the Christ against culture approach becomes "prooftexting." Particular key verses must be satisfied independently of anything else that is said in the Bible. I am reminded here of the Reformation debate over whether the Communion bread actually becomes the physical body of Christ. One side just repeated the scripture that says, "This is my body. Take and eat" (Matthew 26:26). The other side said that this scripture was, like some other scriptures, symbolic rather than literal, and so just quoting that one verse without considering the broader issues was prooftexting.

At the other extreme is religion of culture, when the culture becomes so dominant that spirituality is rewritten in whatever manner culture finds convenient. Jones (1986b) notes people go one step further to reject some spiritualities completely so that any integration is held to be inappropriate. This includes antiintegration psychologists, who hold that it is impossible to be a true psychologist while accepting some "silly superstition like Christianity," a clear case of culture taking precedence over religion.

In the religion of culture approach people use science in a proof–texting manner. Those who hold evolution is completely and totally true (rather than a theory that, as is true of most theories, does not fit all the data) may use it as the criterion for all truth. They may choose a quote here or there that supports their position and ignore the rest. Spirituality must then conform to that position, and anything that disagrees with the position is automatically rejected. That too is inappropriate.

Niebuhr's third category is "religion and culture in paradox." Here the two areas are kept completely compartmentalized. What happens in one is not related to what happens in the other. As Tertullian, a second-century theologian, says, "What has Jerusalem to do with Athens, the church with the academy?" (quoted in Clayton, 1989, p. 9; Dueck, 1995). Each goes its own way. In this case there is no integration to be discussed. Obviously, anyone who writes a book on integration rejects this position.

In addition to the three models already noted, Niebuhr proposed two models of religion and culture in dialogue. These hold that both have value while both are separate disciplines. Theology and Christianity do not dictate to philosophy and psychology, and likewise psychology and philosophy do not dictate to theology and Christianity. However, they are not compartmentalized. Instead, there is active dialogue on issues of relevance to both, and such dialogue means there are open discussions, open arguments, and open debates. There is no assumption that one side will be translated into the other side, or that they will be in perfect agreement. Indeed, one side may even reject part of the other.

Fleck and Carter (1981) give a good overview of early models of integration of psychology and religion used in the psychological literature. They point out that the term "integration" is used in the literature as a casual term. It is not be confused with fusing psychology and the other disciplines together, nor with "psychologizing" Christianity, nor with "Christianizing" psychology. Neither is integration simply aligning terms to match so that the language of one discipline can be translated into the other.

Carter (1977), Larzelere (1980), Crabb (1977), and Jones (1986a) are all among those who have approached integration of psychology and Christian theology in a manner similar to that of the Niebuhr model, albeit in more detail and from several perspectives. Carter identifies models by which psychology may approach theology, as well as other models by which theology might approach psychology. Larzelere considers how integration may take place at different levels, ranging from worldviews to admissible data. Jones presents and critiques several notions of integration that Christians have had. These are worthwhile for more explicit models that particular tasks may require. Carter and Mohline (1976) take the notion of integration further by considering the scopes of theology and of psychology and examining the implications for integration. Bradley identifies six models of integration, as well as problems to avoid, such as not coming to grips with postmod–ernism and being "too theoretical" (which this project tries to avoid in Parts II and III). These also provide references to earlier discussions of integration.

Ellens (1982) and Farnsworth (1985) have proposed a "perspective" model where psychology and Christianity are seen as equal and separate and each examines the other from its own perspective. Tan (1991), on the other hand, suggests that such a model is inappropriate because we stand under the authority of Scripture. However, the perspective model holds the disciplines too far apart, while Tan's "everything is under the authority of Scripture" is incorporated into my definition of Christian theology and could be misinterpreted to deny the value of learning from science. In integration, one discovers areas where one discipline is more relevant than another and uses the discipline accordingly, but everyone should be doing this under the authority of his or her own spirituality and not under dictation from that spirituality. The references in this and the proceeding paragraph are also excellent in examining the critiques that conservative Christians have had of the integration process.

Models upon models upon models have been proposed. Fortunately, Eck (1996) has created a model of models. He identifies underlying processes, such as admissible data. The fact that he works from twenty-seven different models indicates that the references and discussion here just give some hints of what this literature is about. I confess that I am interested in these models at only two points. First, they indicate that there is a variety of ways to integrate disciplines but that "spirituality over culture" or "culture over spirituality" is excluded as integration for most of the models and for this project. Second, they are a literature unto themselves in the sense that few integration projects have started with or been stimulated by the models. Nor have I found them useful to this project beyond the first point made. But if you feel these models will be useful to you, the references here, including Jones (1986a) and Eck (1996) as overviews, will be of interest to you.

Note that different models for integration can be useful at different times. Absolutizing "a model" of integration would artificially restrict dialogues among disciplines. Instead, different models may be called upon in different contexts. When it comes to driving a car, I look mostly to cultural models involving physics and engineering, geography, and both cultural mores and laws (although there are elements of Christian ethics involved too). When it comes to interpersonal relationships, I look to Biblical bases and psychology. When it comes to setting criteria for personal growth, I look to both psychology and spirituality, with the former providing more on methods than goals and the latter providing more on goals than methods. Of course, for a Christian the goal is for Christianity to be involved throughout one's life, since it is the ultimate commitment. Multiple models can be used for integration, and integration need not be just one model.

CRITERIA FOR GOOD INTEGRATION MODELS

From the very brief perusal of models in the last section, it is apparent that people use the term "integration" with different models, and thus in different ways at different times. How then are we to judge what is a good model for integration and what is not?

Integration is not a term that solely involves psychology and philosophy or theology. Instead, integration can involve almost any discipline. Hence, a proper understanding of integration should apply to other disciplines than just psychology and theology. To the degree that an approach to integration does apply more broadly, that will be a better model.

Considering how to evaluate models for integration does not, however, mean that one should have only one model. The works on integration noted here have presented several different models. We will casually shift back and forth between several models throughout this book. Indeed, it may be only after you have read the book that we can really sit down, examine models that have been useful, and then discuss integration models and criteria for integration models. The current discussion is to give us a common orientation at the start of our task.

To further explore the notion of integration, let us consider two examples, one where integration was a focus and another where it was incomplete. Exhibit 1.1 presents the first case, which comes from the history of science and portrays one scientist's view of his work as integration.

Exhibit 1.1
What Was the Purpose of Newton's *Principia*?

Newton's *Principia* (1726/1990) is generally seen as the prime example of a mechanistic universe. An example of a mechanistic model is that of a clock. Once it is constructed and started, all of its movements are determined by the mechanisms of physics. Such a universe may have, as we would see it, little place for God except as a "prime creator and mover" to build and start it. But was this what Newton was about?

Simpson (1992) has examined Newton's works from a historian's perspective. He suggests that Newton saw himself heavily involved in integration; namely, the integration of physics with theology in order to show that the universe was best understood as living forces. Newton felt these forces theologically showed the work of God actively engaged in this world. The fact that this is not a popular interpretation of Newton is blamed by Simpson on a change in paradigms by which people read Newton and the fact that Newton's books are so big. Few people reach the last of his third volume of *Principia*, in which Newton draws his theological conclusions.

In the last section, Newton notes that there are "basic forces" that hold the universe together. Some of these forces, such as gravity, Newton describes in detail and, according to Newton, show God's dominion.

It seems that to Newton the importance of studying gravity was that it was a powerful force that holds the universe together and yet has no underlying physical mechanism for that action. "Gravitons" are the "substance" by which "gravity waves" have their impact, but such have not yet been found except for the single effect of gravity itself. There are no particles, no waves as in the ocean, nothing but space between planets. Yet gravity still works.

It seems strange to us to consider a force that has nothing material found by which the energy is transferred. Moreover, it may violate the principle that nothing exceeds the speed of light (Van Flanders, 1993; for a less technical but open discussion, see Kooistra, 1997).

In addition, Newton saw gravity as God's action or "dominion," that is, God holding the universe together. Newton's conclusion in Volume 3 is, "And from his true dominion it follows that the true God is a living, intelligent, and powerful Being" (Simpson, 1992, p. 165). Simpson suggests that Newton's motivation for his work was to demonstrate God's activity in the current world.

Commentary: There are two levels of integration in this example. First is Newton's theological drive to use knowledge of the physical world to help us understand God's activity in this world. He was serving God through his mathematical and scientific work, not just because it is good to know more, and so we do science. Rather, the science is done to know God better and to prove what God is like, thus answering a theological question.

The second level of integration is Simpson as historian. He not only is bringing together straight "historical facts" of Newton's life and writings, but is also ranging across disciplines requiring understanding of physics, mathematics, and theology. The conclusions range equally broadly. The article could be argued to be appropriate for publication in almost any of those areas.

Why is Exhibit 1.1 integration? Because Newton saw his works simultaneously from two disciplinary perspectives, the sciences and theology. And it was not just theology motivating his being a good scientist; the integration was at a deeper level than that because his question was theological.

Many Christians do, of course, see their work as ministry and serving God. Are they therefore integrating in the sense we use in this book? Perhaps it is personal and implicit integration. However, is there a considered, thoughtful, studied integration? Sometimes that happens and sometimes it does not (see Exhibit 1.2).

Exhibit 1.2
Partial Integration:
Medical Missionaries and the Population Explosion

The New Testament tells us to "heal the sick" (Matthew 10:8) and includes Jesus's statement that "as you did it unto one of the least of these my brethren, so you did it unto me" (Matthew 25:40). Medical missionaries have responded to these verses about healing with some potentially disastrous results, since they seldom integrated with other areas.

The motivation of medical missionaries has been that of a high call. These people, with doctorates in medicine and only casually involved in direct evangelism, have been motivated by the best of Christian love, wanting to ease pain even where the people cannot pay for the medical help they need. In addition, medical missionaries have "healed the sick" and "done it unto the least of these" in a way that other Christians admire. Nothing is to be taken away from that.

However, there seems to have been too little thought given to the outcome of their activities. For while such dedicated Christians reduced the death rate, most failed to equally reduce the birth rate. The result has been overpopulation and the pollution it generates (Howard, 1993).

In countries where medical missionaries have been sent, we now see people fighting for living space. The wars of Africa can be interpreted as wars caused by too little land to support all the people. In addition, the destruction of habitat such as rain forests is caused by the number of people being too great for what the land can carry.

Commentary: What is the integration problem here? No attempt was made to understand the impact of the Christian medical acts in the context of the culture and the carrying capacity of the land. The fact is that few church groups recognize population problems, nor that resource studies show that we have generously fulfilled the Old Testament's first commandment, to "fill the earth" (Genesis 1:28). We are, of course, now sending agricultural developers overseas, but isn't that a couple of decades late? In addition, does it prepare the way for more population growth so that we will be in the same position twenty years from now? What does God call us to do about population?

A more integrated approach is shown by some medical missionaries. For example, Edwin McDaniel was a medical missionary in Chiang Mai, Thailand. He recognized the problem and helped Thailand become concerned about family planning. Thailand is now one of the leaders in controlled population growth. It is too bad that many churches have yet to discuss the commandment to "fill the earth" and what is to be done now that the commandment is fulfilled. McDaniel's example shows that we can heal people at the same time we help them plan for children who can thrive and live a full life without starving or ruining the environment.

Exhibits 1.1 and 1.2 underscore that integration is intrinsically a process, rather than a noun or accomplishment. It means that we bring together the best of theology, philosophy, psychology, and any other relevant disciplines by using the detailed knowledge of those disciplines. In addition, it means that the continual changes of each discipline may, at any time, require reopening integration we thought was safely done. This is a tough requirement for any single scholar.

The time will come when the best integration will be by teams rather than by individuals. At Fuller Theological Seminary we have a start on this because we have had courses taught by two professors, one from psychology and one from theology and missions. Brown, Murphy, and Malony's (1998) "Whatever Happened to the Soul?" is an outgrowth of such endeavors, bringing together psychology, philosophy, and theology. Only a committed administration and faculty has enabled this to happen. It has not been perfect, for we find it easier to teach some aspects of our own discipline than to engage in a true dialog. Unfortunately, the infrastructure to accomplish multidisciplinary integration at a level more than just joint teaching is not yet in sight.

What then of our concept of integration? **For the purposes of this book, integration of psychology and spirituality occurs when psychology and a discipline concerned with spirituality (including philosophy, theology, and ethics) are simultaneously in dialogue to address a question**. By psychology, theology, philosophy, and ethics, we mean the disciplines of each. The phrase "address a question" means that there is a theoretical or applied question that needs answering. Moreover, since it is an activity, we must see it in action. Any activity meeting these criteria is integration. (There is other Christian integration than that which this book is about, but some limits must be placed on every task. These are the limits for this project.)

Earlier I suggested that our approach to integration would need to allow the term to be usable in other contexts, which will reduce the likelihood that our usage misleads the casual reader or general public. Does the previous paragraph meet that objective? What are its implications?

If we think of integrating chemistry and physics, or biology and medicine, or medicine and physics, then the expertise of both disciplines are involved. But does anyone see using engineering to build an ambulance that could carry injured people to hospitals as requiring integration? Would we not expect integration of physics and medicine to be a more appropriate term when using a special physical attribute of blood in developing a new vaccine? The former requires little dialogue; one takes "off the shelf" engineering and builds the ambulance. However, in the latter, experts in both disciplines would be needed. When the technique is in place it becomes a medical technique that involved physics in its development. Note the past tense of the last sentence; there is no active integration because there is no current dialogue. (Again, this limit on the meaning of integration is for the purposes of this book.)

EXERCISE

How do your examples of good and poor integration from the first exercise fit with this approach?

Perhaps at this point you will be seeing integration as a rather large task. That is my opinion: It is a large but important task. It lies at the heart of being a scientist who maximizes his or her impact on the discipline for the good, at the heart of being a therapist who helps others recover and enriches others as well as himself or herself, and it lies at the heart of being an effective person. That also makes it a life-long task. Nevertheless, there are also points of integration that are more easily resolved, and where a thoughtful decision will form a solid basis for one area of life. That too is good; we must not value our integration dialogue so highly that we never get around to using the results to help others.

TWO TYPES OF INTEGRATION
FOR PSYCHOLOGY AND SPIRITUALITY

Integration of several disciplines will occur on different levels and in different places depending on the state of development of those disciplines. For present purposes it is useful to separate two types of integration between psychology and philosophy or theology. The first type occurs at the interdisciplinary interface. It is concerned with commentary—hopefully with a positive attitude—of one discipline on the other discipline, and vice versa. We shall use it in Part II. The second type of integration derives from a particular problem that both disciplines join together to solve. We shall use this in Part III. While both types are integration in that a problem is being addressed from two or more disciplines, the parameters for integration differ considerably.

As with any typology, it is a useful heuristic. It suggests areas for integration and ways to approach it. However, any typology can become a box that traps if it is taken too seriously. Integration is not defined by these two types but by the definition given earlier, the joint endeavor of psychology and spirituality. The task need not fit neatly into one of these two types to be integration. Life often gives us materials that involve a mixture of types as well. That is to be expected, and to consider that a problem would be to take types more seriously than I do.

Commentary Integration

Philosophy has a long history of integration with other disciplines because of its role in analyzing the other disciplines. Philosophers have the task of searching the limits of understanding by language and what is meant by that language. They also examine the possibility of the knowledge on which the discipline could be based and how the theoretical structure might be rationally developed. A simple example of such a critique is given in Exhibit 1.3. That critique has no deep philosophical or theological base, but it is in the spirit of a possible philosophical or theological dialogue with psychology. Beliefs in the sense of truth statements are central to human endeavors, and so whenever a psychology has no place for beliefs, philosophy or theology can critique it on that basis.

EXHIBIT 1.3
In What Do You Believe, O Behaviorist?

My mentor in graduate school, Dr. Raymond B. Cattell (hereafter RBC), started his graduate training at a time when mentalism still existed within psychology and became a behaviorist in part as a reaction against that. He was a strict behaviorist. For example, he viewed his famous personality test, the 16 PF, as a behavioral instrument (Cattell, 1965). The testing situation provides a standardized condition, the item the person reads is a standardized stimulus, and then one analyzes the resulting behavior, the selecting of a response. Moreover, because of his behaviorist approach, practically all the items on this test are reports of behavior rather than self-reported evaluations.

As a student, I was interested in religious beliefs as well as motivations and other aspects of psychology in which Dr. Cattell engaged. I remember asking him about the role of beliefs and whether what people believe might influence their behavior. Dr. Cattell leaned back in his chair with his hands behind his head, said "Hmmm," thought a moment, and then said "Oh, Dick . . ." and changed the subject.

A number of years after graduating, we were sitting in his house in Hawaii looking out on a lagoon. I wished to again ask him about the possible role of beliefs. To better reach a behaviorist such as he, I hypothesized a case of a person drowning in the lagoon and whether a person on the shore might try to swim out to assist. "Surely," I said, "the person's belief in their ability to swim would be important in this decision." Dr. Cattell leaned back in its chair with his hands behind his head, said "Hmmm," thought a moment, and then said "Oh, Dick . . ." and changed the subject.

Commentary: Dr. Cattell was consistent; he was well aware of the paradigm he selected and he operated from it by habit. A strong paradigm behaviorist does not think in mental categories. Therefore, the question of beliefs was outside of his psychological categories.

For me, a major limitation of behaviorism that any theology could quickly point out—which has now been widely acknowledged in psychology by the growth of cognitive psychology as a corrective—was its lack of ability to deal with the intellectual complexity of people. Despite my own tendencies toward behaviorism, my theology holds that beliefs are of great importance. Operating strictly as a psychologist, I am willing to test whether a person's stated beliefs will increase predictions of their behaviors. I now feel that we have enough data to say that beliefs operationalized in such a fashion aid in predicting behavior.

What if beliefs did not predict behavior? Given my theology, I would (and have) conducted psychological research to find out how beliefs can be made to shape behavior.

Psychology has had several theological commentaries on what it has been doing. These range from rejecting psychology as a secular task and therefore not of interest to "true" Christians to encouraging psychology to expand its base to include areas such as religion (see Vitz, 1977). Others, such as Browning (1987), have addressed the issue of how psychological cultures can have assumptions and practices that they may not realize.

The fact that philosophy and theology may critique psychology does not mean that dialogue can only be from philosophy and theology to other areas. Commentary can go either way. The question depends only upon whether a discipline has a question to ask or suggestion to make about the assumptions or methodologies of the other discipline.

Moreover, psychology does have some suggestions for philosophy and theology. Let's consider one example here. Social psychology has long found that leadership is exerted by an individual on a group only after the leader has been accepted as a member within the group. To be accepted as a leader within a group, the individual must contribute greatly to the group and obviously hold to the group's norms.

Social psychology's view of who can lead a group is in direct conflict to some opinions about how scientific and theological revolutions occur. Many graduate students arrive with the impression that it is the new person, or the person outside of the field and its current paradigms, that is able to see its limitations, develop better theories than those held by the "establishment," and change the field. This would be strange indeed, given our knowledge of group dynamics from social psychology.

Exhibit 1.4 suggests that the idea that discipline revolutions come from new people is false. It is, instead, the individuals established within the current paradigm who are able to overthrow that paradigm. So, if you do not have solid publications that demonstrate that you know what you and the discipline are talking about, expect to be ignored if you attempt to criticize that area. You have to prove that you can do the paradigm before people will feel that you know enough to revise it.

EXHIBIT 1.4
When Do Leaders Make Their Major Contributions?

To gain a decent sample and have a somewhat objective method for determining when major leaders in science and related areas have made their contribution, I turned to the *Great Books of the Western World* (Goetz, 1990). The appearance of individuals in that series signifies that they were indeed seen as leaders and that their publications still have an impact in defining the paradigms of an area, at least in a historical if not a current sense. The age of each person's "greatest contribution" was taken from the introduction to that person's work in the *Great Books*. Here is the list and the age of each scientist's most important contribution:

Scientist	Age	Criterion
Copernicus	36	First publication
Darwin	50	*Origin of Species*
Galileo	45	"Most famous discovery"
Harvey	50	Circulation of blood
Kepler	45	"Most important work"
Newton	45	*Mathematical Principles*
Pascal	28	Law of Hydrodynamics

It is apparent that most revolutionaries were neither young nor new to their fields. In fact, it seems that they were generally in their field for fifteen years or more before their revolutionary work. Most of the people in this list had impressive early publications as well. However, these were from within the paradigm, not challenging it.

The possible exception to long-term involvement with one's field is Pascal, but note two facts regarding his career. First, he died at thirty-nine; some hold that he would have made even greater contributions if he had lived longer. Second, he had known for years the fields of his greatest contributions. While still a lad, his father took him to meetings of philosophical societies; this was so successful that his father forbade his studying geometry until he became sixteen. So he derived much of it on his own. If you count his early teens as his entry point into the field, then he too had years of experience when he made his major contribution.

Commentary: These results are as predicted from the social psychological research on groups and leadership.

While Exhibit 1.4 is an example of historical data, it also illustrates how data about people—generally found in psychology per se—may contribute to our understanding of the processes that impact what happens. Both cognitive psychology and social psychology are very active in this area (e.g., Bar-Tel & Kruglanski, 1988; O'Donohue & Kitchner, 1996; Shadish & Fuller, 1994).

Integration as Joint Problem Solving

In addition to one discipline helping another through commentary, integration takes place around joint problem solving. In contrast to Commentary Integration, Joint Problem Solving is focused on the cooperative application of the disciplines to accomplish a goal. The problem may arise in either of the two disciplines. For example, since psychology as a science has little to say about values, it is not unusual for theology to set a goal that psychology then helps achieve. Or Christian clinical psychologists may turn to theologians for guidance on issues such as divorce, justice, abortion, homosexuality, and neurotic versus true guilt.

Francis and Jones (1996) have edited a book of papers all concerned with the effectiveness of ministry, which is the "problem" being addressed. The context and goals are defined by the churches and provide the basic goals, values, and context. The papers use social science techniques and theories to examine, among other topics, expectations, stress, and burnout. Hill and Butter (1995) are concerned with health and how spiritual practices might enhance it. Both involve joint problem solving; both need input from two disciplines to reach the best conclusions.

Joint Problem Solving Integration has historically been the primary focus integrating clinical psychology and theology (see Chapter 6). A major "problem" has been that of mental disorders, and the help has been that of providing mental health services to clergy or laity. Mostly this integration has been Christian leaders setting up a system with psychologists to assure that people who need care receive care.

When is it integration to send a clergyperson to a therapist to help them, for example, adjust to the stresses of ministry? We noted earlier that just the use of another discipline is not necessarily integration. It only becomes integration, in the present use of the term, when both disciplines are actively engaged.

Clinical psychology and theology are both actively engaged when therapy is different because of the theology. This means that both psychology and philosophy or theology are engaged within the therapy session. Note that this goes beyond therapy by a Christian psychologist to therapy by an integrated Christian psychologist. Hence, the extensive literature on religion and clinical psychology is, for our purposes, in need of separation. That part that improves clinical psychology in general is not integration, but the part that engages in theological issues, such as ethics, would be integration. (Clinical psychology integration is discussed more in Chapter 6.)

Other possibilities for joint problem solving exist. Some of these revolve around issues of how the Church can accomplish its goals better. Exhibit 1.5 is an example. Other examples include the development of procedures to help clergy (Hunt, 1991; Malony, 1988) or to help select and develop people to start new churches (Mebane & Ridley, 1988).

EXHIBIT 1.5
Lay Counseling in Church Settings

Many people could benefit from the help that counseling provides. Many of these do not need therapists with the in-depth training of a Ph.D. or even of an M.A. This is true with church people as well as others, but the need in some churches is slightly greater than would be expected. It seems that some Christians have learned of therapists who did not respect the religiousness of the clients or of "marriage" counselors who actually turned out to be "divorce" counselors. These people want a therapist who is a Christian, and, without such, they are uncounseled.

In response to such needs, Siang-Yang Tan (1991) has developed special programs to train lay people for counseling in churches. The churches provide the settings and the laity to be trained. They also support the counseling of the trained laity. Here is how Dr. Tan sees this as integration in his book, *Lay Counseling: Equipping Christians for a Helping Ministry.* First the Bible calls us to "bear one another's burdens" (Galatians 6:2), and Jesus models a dynamic caring. Spiritual gifts in admonishing, encouraging, and helping others are to be used in our ministry one to another. Psychological principles that are "consistent with Scripture, hence subjecting them to the authority of Scripture" (Tan, 1991, p. 32) enable lay people to more effectively use their spiritual gifts to fulfill their calling.

Commentary: Tan's (1991) presentation is integration since the program requires consistent attention both to Scripture and to psychology. The basic question and the limits of what should or should not be done come from Biblical theology. Psychology fills in the details. For example, in discussing how people should be supervised, Tan notes supervision styles identified in clinical research as psychologically inappropriate; this knowledge guides the spiritually mature supervisor away from psychologically poor styles.

The brief examples here (with more to be explored later) have so far been of the Church's need for psychology. However, the needs go in the other direction as well, particularly in an area such as clinical psychology. What is a "good outcome" when counseling a marriage in trouble? How much effort should be made to keep the couple together? What are the ethical issues for a Christian in counseling gays and lesbians? Is homosexuality a sin? If so, is it a strong sin or a weak sin (with "weak sin" being one to which we give "lip service" but really feel it is virtually impossible to avoid and so is "understandable")? In addition, how is therapy done when Christian norms depart from the norms of the society that provides the therapist's license and may, through insurance or grant programs, fund the therapy?

The brief examples so far have been of integrating psychology with philosophy and theology or the Church, but there is a wide range of possibilities that may include other disciplines. Exhibit 1.6 is one example. The problem raised there can only be answered by combining the expertise of both Church history and psychology. Such areas can be expected to grow as the examples of successful integration stimulate the disciplines.

Exhibit 1.6
What Changed the Nature of Church Debates
from A.D. 950 to 1050?

Psychologists have studied methods of reasoning, with each method being a qualitatively different approach. This study of reasoning has been primarily as developmental stages and the basics have been widely replicated. Thus McDougell (1908) produced approaches (or modes or stages) that are very close to what others (e.g., Peck & Havighurst, 1960; Bull, 1969) have identified and those that have been adapted to moral education (e.g., Kohlberg, 1969). While most of the work has examined the changes in approaches to reasoning as a child develops—and so has labeled stages—multiple approaches are found in adults (see Gilligan, 1988, for variations across adults missed by earlier investigators).

Such differences in reasoning can be seen in theological debates in England. Toward the end of the Middle Ages (e.g., A.D. 900–950), the theological debates about the causes of illness were "quoting contests" (Slack, 1985). Each of the debaters listed everything that could be found to support his or her position. The quotes might be from Church fathers, respected philosophers, or the Bible. These were in no particular order; that is, they were not organized around themes but seem to a modern reader to be in random order. The opposing debaters gave their list of quotes (I do not know if the winner was decided by the length of the list, the fame of those being quoted, or some other principle).

From a psychological perspective and to use Piaget categories (Darley, Glucksberg, & Kinchla, 1988), these debates are examples of preabstract thinking (and probably even preconcrete operations thinking). Without the use of abstract thinking, there is little way in which materials can be organized. Abstract thinking is a necessary prerequisite to logical organization of materials.

However, the debates were different 100 years later. By A.D.1050 the debaters presented their rationales by logical, abstract reasoning (Slack, 1985), just as do current thinkers.

Commentary: The questions for Church historians and psychologists include the following: What happened to change the mode of reasoning of a culture in just 100 years? What kept the mode so low during the "Dark Ages"? An understanding of the church history of that period needs to involve the psychology of types of thinking.

EXERCISE

Which type of integration are your example(s) from the first exercise closest to? What is the relationship of each to the models of Christ and culture? Is either an example of Commentary or of Joint Problem Solving Integration?

INTEGRATION AS PERSONAL

The materials already presented show professional integration. Personal integration also occurs. **Personal integration occurs when people make their personal decisions based on the disciplines of both psychology and spirituality.** It is a situationally specific process and goal.

As a term in this book, "personal integration" is reserved for the impact of integration upon other than professional decisions. Professional decisions include evaluating the evidence for theory X versus theory Y and deciding what treatment should be given for a particular diagnosis. However, living within a profession will also involve personal issues, as in how we treat a person of another ethnicity. Bufford (1997) makes this point by noting that the distinctiveness of Christian counseling is found in the counselor.

Personal and professional integration are not mutually exclusive, and decisions may involve both. Do we involve both our psychology and our theology when we are falling asleep in committee meetings? In deciding who our friends will be or who we will offer to support financially? Do we use both to shape our devotional lives? Exhibit 1.7 suggests what is truly important in people's lives is personal integration, and being a psychologist or theologian does not negate that.

Exhibit 1.7
Is the Personal Level Important?

Passages of Scripture that we find very important generally happen at the personal level rather than the disciplinary level. Consider the parables. Many of them are like the Parable of the Prodigal Son (Luke 15:11–32), which happen in family events among people deeply and intimately related to each other. Others, such as the Parable of the Good Samaritan (Luke 10:29–37), happen between strangers. Nevertheless, each carries a clear message: Christianity is about living the faith in everyday, personal situations.

Consider the report of Jesus's encounter with the Samaritan woman at the well (John 4:7–30). Jesus violated customs of cultural segregation by asking her for a drink of water, and then proceeded to surprise her by his knowledge of her having had many husbands and her currently living with a man who was not her husband. Perhaps even more surprising was that he spent time talking to such an obviously sinful person. And he offered her hope and a chance for a new life. Jesus's actions involved psychological, cultural, and theological understandings, but they were applied at a very personal level. After all, how much more personal can you get than discussing someone's sexual history and sharing a drink of water together?

Here is another example of personal integration. Dr. Raymond B. Cattell argued for years that intelligence is one of the most important characteristics of humanity. He also reported data that bright and well-educated people are not having enough children to maintain their proportion in the total population. Dr. Cattell also knew he himself to be a bright and well-educated person. Therefore, he had five children. This is about as personal as it gets.

Personal integration is an existential task and happens in specific situations. These multiple possible integrative events are points along the journey that makes up a life. Whether or not they are integrative experiences depends on whether we use psychology and theology jointly to guide our lives. Do we require them to dialogue within us?

Because most integration includes personal integration, this book is occasionally more personal than a standard book. I cannot write it without sharing some personal stories and narratives that, hopefully, shed some light on the task of integration. I already began this when reporting my questions to my mentor about beliefs, and shall occasionally do so throughout the text. This is not to say that my integration is any better than another's, but it is what I know best. Perhaps we can all learn from it.

As part of my sharing, the work of my students will be occasionally used as illustrations. This is in part because I know it well, but it is also in part because of my own integration journey. My research involvements have been in part due to my integration goals and in part because God was preparing me for a role that I did not anticipate. To put it another way, scholars who don't think some of their own research is valuable enough to quote should never have done that research. For better or for worse, I feel that some of the work I have done is what the field should have been doing, and I shall, as a part of sharing a little of my personal integration, occasionally explain the reasons why.

I shall not restrict examples of integration to my personal journey, but shall also involve others. The other person who will most often appear is Dr. Raymond B. Cattell. He was my mentor in graduate school and I have had occasional professional interactions with him over the years. However, the most important reason we shall be writing of him is that he is one of the most integrated scientists I have known. He has written not only his scientific contributions but also on the relationships between psychology and society (including religion and ethics). A source for other examples of personal integration among psychologists is Hoshmand (1999), which includes narratives by and about seven other psychologists, although the integration is casual. Malony (1978) has articles from eighteen Christian psychologists about their integration journeys.

RBC's integration is also useful to us for another reason. Most integration has been done by Christians, as is this book. However, RBC rejected all of the world's religions in favor of being a Darwinist and following an approach he calls "Beyondism" (Cattell, 1987). Hence he approached integration from a different perspective and, while I strongly disagree with him at particular points, his work provides that additional insight that can occur from "seeing how someone outside the fold does it."

EXERCISE

Explain how your examples in the first exercise may include personal integration. If they do not, could the personal be involved in your "excellent integration" case?

OUTLINE OF THE PROJECT

This first chapter has provided some definitions of psychology and spirituality and then pointed to classical models of integration and outlined two types of professional integration. It has also clearly stated that personal integration is needed as well as professional. These discussions provide the working notions of the kinds of integration that this book addresses.

Since integration involves contributions from several disciplines, one task is to establish how those disciplines come to decisions and how they fit together. This is the task in Chapter 2, where we consider the relationships among the sciences (psychology) and humanities (theology, philosophy, ethics). This cannot be in the abstract but must include the contexts of the sciences and the humanities in general. We shall pay particular attention to the changing role of psychology relative to other disciplines, the ways in which science and the humanities might be considered to produce knowledge, and the differences between professional and personal integration.

We cannot integrate that which we do not know, and understanding the nature of integration is our first task. Upon understanding the nature of each discipline, our knowledge as psychologists can be put to good effect integrating psychology with spirituality. (For psychology already integrated with Christianity, see such references as Faw, 1995; Fleck & Carter, 1981; Jones, 1986a; Tan, 1991; they devote the majority of their space to that material). The use of Christian theology as my base will also, I hope, give illustrations about the nature of integration itself as well as what the Christian faith may have to contribute. Non-Christian spirituality is also occasionally used, since this project is not limited to Christianity per se.

Part II begins integration with Commentary Integration. Given the nature of the several disciplines, what can those concerned with science, particularly psychology, say to those concerned with spirituality? And what might spirituality say to psychologists?

Knowing what disciplines bring to integration allows Chapters 3 and 4 to address broader questions of how we reach integrated decisions as integrated people. Spirituality starts us out by commenting on what it finds to be the limits of science in Chapter 3. The role of personal experience as a basis for actual decision making, the problem of free will versus determinism, and the problem of evil are included. These are examples of issues that spirituality points to that scientists need to consider, both for scientific disciplines themselves and for personal integration.

Chapter 4 reverses the integrative question by asking for psychology's commentary on discussions in spirituality. Much of what is said in this chapter comes from what we know of human decision making. It ranges from, on the one hand, resources for nonpsychology scholars concerned with spirituality that can help them to find well-established knowledge in psychology which might be relevant to their tasks, to, on the other hand, how psychology might be used to develop interventions to enhance spiritual development.

Part III gives some examples of Joint Problem Solving Integration. The chapters of Part III look at integration with particular areas of psychology. The questions include to what extent these areas have already been involved in integration and some examples of what they have to offer. The goal is to stimulate questions about how contemporary psychology may contribute to integration. This part is neither comprehensive nor exhaustive; there are many more problems that could be addressed jointly. Hopefully these examples will stimulate dialogue between disciplines to enhance joint problem solving.

Clinical psychology is concerned with many issues that may best be jointly addressed by both psychology and spirituality (Chapter 5). These issues include the question of what the final goal of therapy should be, the appropriate training of clinical psychologists to deal with spirituality, and the use of spiritual resources to enhance therapy.

Social psychology is the focus of Chapter 6 because of its great potential for coaddressing issues with spirituality. The causes of and interventions to reduce conflict and prejudice are prime foci. Hopefully these areas will be effective examples that stimulate interest in integrating spirituality and social psychology for joint problem solving.

The progression of topics leaves many interesting spiritual issues to the later chapters instead of setting forth my spirituality and theological assumptions first and examining psychology in the light of those assumptions. This is a deliberate choice arising from the fact that neither those concerned with spirituality nor psychologists necessarily work from a Christian or other religious base. This book is written for both Christians and non-Christians. This approach also reminds us that the contributions of non-Christians in those areas may be useful to Christians as well. Therefore, the first chapters are designed to examine these disciplines in their secular forms. The relating of secular psychology and philosophy to theology then flows from a basic understanding of what each discipline can say to each other.

This book is by a single author, which has the advantage of greater consistency than a multiauthored book. However, it has the disadvantage that no one can be expert in all psychology that might be relevant to integration. And even if that were the case, there is too much good material in psychology to be reduced to one book. Hence, be warned that this book is the result of my journey and the psychology I know and feel is important. Many of the principles I will mention are those, like in Exhibit 1.6, that are well established over decades of research but are not necessarily current "hot topics." Therefore, you will not see many references to recent journal articles, for I look for principles that are so basic that they must be included regardless of recent interest. Hopefully such examples will stimulate you in your journey to integrate psychology with spirituality.

EXERCISE

For which chapter of the book could your examples from the first exercise be used? Do you have examples that might fit another area of integration?

Cosgrove, M., & Mallory, J. (1977). Mental health: A Christian perspective. Grand Rapids, MI: Zondervan.

Crabb, L. J., Jr. (1977). Effective biblical counseling: A model of helping caring Christians become capable counselors. Grand Rapids, MI: Zondervan.

Dueck, A. C. (1995). Between Jerusalem and Athens. Grand Rapids, MI: Baker Books.

Ellison, C. (1994). From stress to well being. Dallas, TX: Word.

Hurding, R. (1992). The Bible and counseling. London: Hodder and Stoughton.

Jones, S. L., & Butman, R. E. (1991). Modern psychotherapies: A comprehensive Christian appraisal. Downers Grove, IL: InterVarsity Press.

Lovinger, R. J. (1984). Working with religious issues in therapy. New York: Jason Aronson.

Lovinger, R. J. (1990). Religion and counseling: The psychological impact of religious belief. New York: Continuum.

Malony, H. N. (1983). Wholeness and holiness: Readings in the psychology and theology of mental health. Grand Rapids, MI: Baker.

Malcmoto, C. (1992). The scandal of psychotherapy. Wheaton, IL: Tyndale.

McMinn, M. R. (1996). Psychology, theology, and spirituality in Christian counseling. Wheaton, IL: Tyndale House.

Meier, P., Minirth, F., Wichern, F., & Ratcliff, D. (1991). Introduction to psychology and counseling. Grand Rapids, MI: Baker.

Miller, W. R. (Ed.). (1999). Integrating spirituality into treatment. Washington, DC: American Psychological Association.

Miller, W. R., & Martin, J. E. (Eds.). (1988). Behavior therapy and religion: Integrating spiritual and behavioral approaches to change. Newbury Park, CA: Sage.

Richards, P. S., & Bergin, A. E. (Eds.). (1997). A spiritual strategy for counseling and psychotherapy. Washington, DC: American Psychological Association.

Sanders, R. K. (Ed.) (1997). Christian counseling ethics: A handbook for therapists, pastors, & counselors. Downers Grove, IL: InterVarsity Press.

Shafranske, E. P. (Ed.) (1996). Religion and the clinical practice of psychology. Washington, DC: American Psychological Association.

Southard, S. (1972). Christians and mental health. Nashville: Broadman.

Southard, S. (1969). Theology and therapy. Dallas, TX: Word.

Stern, E. M. (Ed.). (1985). Psychotherapy and the religiously committed patient. New York: Haworth.

Tan, S. Y. (1991). Lay counseling: Equipping Christians for a helping ministry. Grand Rapids, MI: Zondervan.

Tjeltveit, A. (1999). Ethics and values in psychotherapy. New York: Routledge.

CHAPTER 2

Relationships among Disciplines

To integrate psychology and spirituality it is useful to understand the nature of science and humanities because psychology is a part of the former and spirituality is a part of the former. We begin that understanding by noting a classical pyramid of disciplines of science, wherein physics is seen as both the basis and the prototype of all science. What do terms such as fact, objectivity, and theory mean? How does psychology fit into this?

The classical chart, however, is unclear about one element that is crucial for our discussions. That element is the basic primacy of philosophy for all the disciplines because of the question of how knowledge in each discipline can be attained. That is not a simple task. The heart of that discussion is one historical, philosophic point that virtually defines the postmodern philosophical era in which we live: Descartes's "Cogito, ergo sum." Many hold this is a critical critique that would invalidate much of the search for all knowledge; to what degree are they correct?

Decisions about knowledge are psychological decisions, so the next section introduces the role psychology must play in the understanding of how disciplines may know what they claim to know. Psychology is the "late bloomer" in this discussion; can we get a glimpse of its possible role?

But what of the spirituality disciplines? Can, for example, theology be said to be concerned with truth that cannot be found via science? Building on the basis of the earlier sections, do the humanities, including theology, have a unique approach to truth? Will integrating this with scientific truth lead to wisdom?

In the last part of this chapter we expand the classical pyramid to bring in our interests in personal as well as professional integration. This is essential to understand what each discipline can and cannot do, where the science paradigm is limited, and whether another knowledge paradigm can be added for personal as well as professional decisions.

THE RELATIONSHIPS AMONG SCIENCES

The following is the classical pyramid of the scientific disciplines (Murphy, 1990; a less classical but perhaps more informative version is Murphy, 1997, ch. 9):

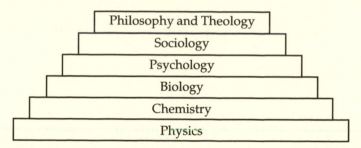

Physics is at the bottom and philosophy and theology are at the top. This list is not quite complete because areas such as political science and astronomy are not included, but it is sufficient for our purposes. By the definition of science developed here, psychology is a science—although a young one—and therefore psychological examples are mixed with those from other sciences.

The pyramid is classically interpreted as illustrating that physics is the foundation of the sciences. Out of physics comes chemistry. If we knew enough physics and wished to do so, chemistry could be written using the terms of physics. In the same manner, biology is a formal development of chemistry and physics. All of biology itself can, in this approach, be rewritten in terms of physics and chemistry. Biological processes using oxygen to produce energy with carbon monoxide as a by-product, for example, would be rewritten in chemistry. Cell structure would be rewritten in physics. Psychology builds directly on biology. Thus, if we do enough biology (and chemistry and physics), everything in psychology could be predicted therefrom. All of psychology could be explained in physiological terms if we knew enough. In addition, sociology builds on psychology.

Perhaps you were surprised to see philosophy and theology at the top of the pyramid. How are they part of science? It is true that some of philosophy and theology are independent of science. However, these two disciplines are concerned about developing totalistic views on the nature of reality. Such views or perspectives must include science, including what science has established. Therefore, these disciplines at the top of the pyramid rely on the disciplines below them, for "data" come from the sciences in addition to their own disciplinary data.

Of course, a person who took the pyramid too seriously might conclude that only those who master physics could understand psychology, or that a well-trained psychologist must know, in extensive detail, physics, chemistry, and biology. Obviously, the pyramid illustration is useful but limited.

Why is the illustration of the pyramid limited? The answer has three parts, one of which is based on logic and the others of which are based on psychology. First, consider this illustration. When the same expression in mathematics occurs multiple times, a label is given to the expression so that a symbol can be used instead of the entire expression. In statistics, we have the expression $Sum(X)/N$ that is replaced by M to stand for the mean. It makes the expressions simpler. In addition, it helps the logic be clear. Therefore, a discipline such as chemistry will have a label, such as "water," which actually is shorthand for the physics description of the molecular structure of hydrogen in combination with oxygen. Alternatively, a psychologist who describes a person as having an IQ of 120 is using, in theory, shorthand for a particular neurological structure and activity. Whether or not the professional needs to know the further specification of water or IQ would depend on the situation. A person investigating the possibility of brain damage would use IQ differently than a career counselor advising a high school student. Thus, the professional can look at phenomena from whichever level is most convenient without being confronted with overwhelming detail.

A second reason for not just doing everything in physics is that the "shorthand" may be what is observed and therefore a direct object of study. Water was observed long before we identified hydrogen and oxygen. To hold up the study of water until physics had identified its molecular structure would have been counterproductive.

A third reason for having the separate disciplines is that it is difficult for one person to understand more than one discipline. Indeed, it is probably impossible for one person to even understand one discipline completely. There is just too much being done. How then could anyone understand both physics and psychology sufficiently to explain psychology in terms of physics?

Other critiques of the classical pyramid have also been proposed. These include the fact that new properties emerge at higher levels that are not predicted from the lower levels. However, proponents of the hierarchical interpretation can note that this is an argument from ignorance. They reply, "as soon as we know enough physics, we will be able to derive that also." Of course, neither side can prove their case so it seem a fruitless discussion.

Each of the areas is inclined to assume that it is the most important. We should not take that too seriously, for this happens within psychology as well (e.g., see Exhibit 2.1) and is a derivative of the "ethnocentric bias" noted later. For integration, we shall assume the disciplines involved are equally important.

EXHIBIT 2.1
Three Views on the True Basis for Psychology

Social Psychology View

Fortunately, we have social psychology to examine that which is of true importance, such as interpersonal relationships and the psychology of spirituality and faith. For example, helping people become more loving is best researched by directly examining the relevant events. Once we understand how the events fit into a process, we can maximize such characteristics as altruism. Since the development of the person is in a social environment, this is the crux of psychology.

Physiological Psychology View

What happens to a person happens physiologically. There is no touch, no movement, no emotion, no thinking, no praying, no anything psychological but what happens with the body. Every new habit is learned through neurological interactions and becomes a habit only as there are physiological changes. Eventually, with enough knowledge, every thought and every movement can be monitored, and then we shall know how the person is and will respond. Every other area of psychology can then be documented and reproduced through physiological psychology, and so this is the only true psychology.

Environmentalist View

That which a person becomes both physiologically and social psychologically is a function of the environment. Food must be ingested for the physiological to happen and a culture must exist for social interactions to develop (and be stored in the physiological structure). Physiological and social psychology are just derivatives of the environment's interaction with the person, so the real work is in the study of that environment.

Commentary: Hopefully you recognized that these examples are caricatures. Nevertheless, note that we are all human and choose our discipline because we think it is important. It is little wonder to find each suggesting that his or her own discipline is the really important one, for who would choose a discipline if they felt it was trivial?

The Nature of Science

The classical science pyramid suggests science to be the basis and the prime content for philosophy and theology. The scientific methods of justification for theories vary as a function of the level of the discipline in the pyramid. In the more basic areas, such as physics and chemistry, justification relies heavily on experimentation. One person develops a research design that tests a particular hypothesis and reports the results. The nature of that report is crucial for understanding the logic of the sciences (Gorsuch, 2002), for the scientific report contains a complete description of how the research was carried out. Therefore, everyone qualified to read the article can personally test whether the results are as stated. In fact, the original meaning of the word "experiment" was very close to what we today refer to as a "demonstration" (*Oxford Universal Dictionary*, 1955, p. 656), and that catches the flavor of the report. It tells how you can demonstrate to yourself and others what the author found.

Note that the "results" section of a published paper are just data summaries, not interpretations. The discussion section then interprets the results. Whether we argue or say the results support theory x or theory y is an entirely different matter from the results per se.

The importance of the scientific report for understanding science cannot be exaggerated (Gorsuch, 2002). Science is based on the ability of anyone trained in a discipline to replicate the results of anyone else. This points to several values in science.

First, the principle that the report must show how to replicate the experiment provides a definition of "fact": **A fact is established when people running the same research procedure get the same results.** A fact is not some "magical" way to "truth" of a radically different nature from the truth of everyday life. A fact is instead based on data consistency; that is, an outcome that occurs when data are collected under the standardized conditions of the experiment. Scientific fact is quite distinct from scientific theory, which is defined later.

Is science objective? **A statement is "objective" to the degree that all qualified people readily agree to it.** In psychology, the degree to which measurement is objective is assessed by rater agreement

(Gorsuch, 2002): The higher the rater agreement, the higher the objectivity. "Subjective" is the opposite of objective, when raters disagree. Combining this definition of objective with the condition for concluding that a fact is established means that scientific facts are objective.

To the degree that something is subjective, its meaningfulness is in question. If it is completely subjective, then by definition no two people can agree on it. If I say "x refers to my experience last night" and you who were also there say "x obviously doesn't apply to that," then we have no rater agreement, no objectivity, and we have to question whether we are using x in the same way.

Of course, most of the time there is some degree of objectivity rather than something being either completely objective or subjective. This is quantified by statistics, such as percentage of agreement. For example, to test the acidity of water, a chemical is added that produces a color. If the water is acidic, it turns pink. If it is alkaline, it turns blue. If it is partly both, the water is some mix of color between those. Raters agree 100 percent of the time when the samples of water are either highly acidic or highly alkaline. But what happens if one sample of water is acidic and the other is almost acidic? The colors are much closer to each other, the judgment is more difficult, and the percentage of agreement drops. When the colors are virtually identical, the raters may only agree at a chance level as to whether the two samples differ.

Is the judgment of the acidity of water objective or subjective? By the first example with only acidic and alkaline samples, it is objective. By the second example, it is subjective. It is a poor question, for the answer depends on how the test is established. It is better to ask if it is *ever* objective, since if it never is, no communication is possible. When the answer to that question is "yes," then ask the conditions under which it is objective.

Vande Kemp (1996) suggests that phenomenology is good because it permits "taking seriously experiences usually dismissed by modern psychologists," such as experiences without external referents. Whether these are science or not depends on how well the investigation can be objective in the sense that others readily agree to it and it can be replicated. Note that whatever part of a phenomenological analysis does not meet the criteria for science is not false or worthless. What it does mean is that it is not appropriate for science.

Can science include qualitative data? The terms "quantitative" and "qualitative" are difficult to clearly define and there is much confusion about their use. I prefer to use them to identify when data form a continuum versus when they are independent, with the former being quantitative and the latter qualitative. Thus, height or intelligence is a quantitative measurement because different heights or intelligences can be positioned along the same continuum, such as the number of meters a person is tall or who is the most intelligent child in the class. But hair color is qualitatively different from height because height and hair color are not directly related on the same scale, just as intelligence is qualitatively different from anxiety. This makes any difference that cannot be scaled in the same metric a qualitative difference. (For the reader acquainted with the statistical technique of factor analysis, in Gorsuch [1983] I consider factor analysis to identify the qualitative differences among the variables being measured. Each factor identifies an area qualitatively different from any other factor.)

However, these definitions of qualitative and quantitative do not seem to represent what many refer to by these terms. Qualitative measurement, for example, seems to mean when descriptive labels are given rather than numbers (Nunnally & Bernstein, 1994). The descriptive labels are at the nominal level of measurement; that is, when it consists of a set of categories (for more information on "nominal measurement," see an introductory measurement or statistics text or Nunnally & Bernstein, 1994). Ethnicity is generally used as a nominal variable. One ethnic group is seen not at some point along a continuum of groups, but as unique.

Classic statistics was built on the quantitative–qualitative difference. The former was represented by parameter statistics such as correlation coefficients and the latter by nonparametric statistics such as the Pierson cross-tab table analysis using chi square. However, we now know that is wrong; we can represent each category of a nominal variable within a multiple regression equation (e.g., Cohen & Cohen, 1983) and analyze it along with data such as height. While we shall not attempt to explain it here, even the "nonparametric" chi square cross-tab analysis is a special case of parameter statistics (Gorsuch, 1990–1999). Indeed, if you can give it a name, we can analyze it as quantitative data—just let its presence be scored 1 and its absence be scored 0. So if two people can agree on when a word is appropriately used to describe anything, it can be treated as quantitative data. With these developments, the classical distinction between qualitative and quantitative disappear and these two terms do not seem to be helpful. Objective and subjective are more useful, since they inform us of the degree of common agreement. The role of the scientific report underscores the value placed by scientists on objective data.

The research report shows a second value of science: the open communication of ideas and procedures. Others have the right to know how to run the same test for themselves.

Third, the science report shows that a community is involved. It is expected that others will be replicating the study, and that the results will only be accepted as fact when that community is convinced by replicating the results.

Exhibit 2.2 contains a case of attempted replication that has not yet worked. Note that the results originally suggested were not rejected simply because most scientists felt those results went against what they thought (although this plays a role in science as community, as discussed later). It was the experience of nonreplication, that following the announced procedures did not lead to the same results. That experience led to the rejection of the claims, and the conclusion that there was no fact. (Friedlander, 1995, is an excellent introduction to science, considering basic cases that are science and cases that someone portrays as science but actually are not science.)

EXHIBIT 2.2
Why Is Cold Fusion Rejected?

Cold fusion was introduced in a press conference with much fanfare in 1989. Fusion had occurred previously in theory and in reports but only at very high temperatures, such as inside a star. So when the scientists thought they had observed fusion at room temperatures, they were excited and introduced their experiment to the public.

The cold fusion experiment was "low tech." Many scientists had the necessary equipment in their laboratories to try the experiment. And many did, but they did not find the same results. Since the results have not yet been generally replicated, cold fusion has not been accepted as scientific fact.

There were other factors involved in scientists' reactions to cold fusion. Scientists challenged the study because they doubted what had happened. These doubts were because the results contradicted other facts, as scientists understood them, about fusion and the theory of fusion. The press reported these doubts often.

For science the rejection was neither because of past research nor because of current theory, but was because other scientists could not replicate the results. Rejection of an experiment may be in part because it violates past research or current theory, but the prime essential is replication (Friedlander, 1995, pp. 27–34).

Might a finding shift from nonreplicable—and hence not a fact—to replicable and hence a fact? Yes, if, for example, a better method is found that produces the same results when tried by others.

An implication of the identification of science with replicable facts is that the definition is very broad. It need not be an intervention by the researcher, nor does it need to involve numbers. It is, for example, broad enough to include phenomenology, as suggested by Vande Kemp (1996, 1998). It can also include analyses of in-depth interviews and other materials such as diaries. For example, an appropriate analysis of cross-cultural values can use common methods but must also use more qualitative methods to include multiple facets of values along with critical thinking to see when the "standard" procedures may come up short. Using multiple methods, Gorsuch and Barnes (1973) found some cross-cultural generalization of moral content and of structure. They also were the first, based on their more ethnographic observations, to point out the individualism of Kohlberg's (1969) stages. These can all be a part of science, as long as the procedure producing the results is published and others following that procedure find the same results.

The replicability of facts is often investigated with experiments, but the term "experiment" can be used in either a strong or a weak manner. The strong sense requires a change introduced by the person running the study. Only a change study (i.e., one with an intervention by the investigators) is thus labeled an experiment. In the weaker usage of the term, "experiment" is used to apply to a standard set of observations under conditions either when the investigator provides the change or when the change is provided by some other agent. In the weak usage, noting the effects of the moon on tidal levels is a fair experiment. Astronomy classically uses experiment in a weaker sense then does physics. However, others restrict the term to only its strong sense—as I generally do—and use a term such as "research study" for other cases. Nevertheless, even for research studies, the principle remains that a fact is declared only when the full methodology is published and someone else replicates the results with that methodology.

What then is theory? A theory is never a fact; instead, **a theory is a convenient way to summarize facts so they can be grasped by our human minds**. Since it is "our human minds," it must make sense to the current generation of thinkers. A new generation may wish to rewrite the theory so "it makes more sense" to them; that is, they rewrite it so it can be grasped by their human minds. Theories are therefore social constructions. Of course, any theory that replaces an older theory does so either because the new theory accounts for more facts or because the new theory is easier to grasp (sometimes referred to as more "elegant"). But the new theory must do as well as the old theory is accounting for the established facts. (A change in theories may well change which facts are seen as relevant and how the facts are described.)

At the bottom of the pyramid of sciences experiment is used in the strong sense, but opportunities for changing conditions become more difficult as we go higher in the pyramid. When psychology is reached, the traditional "pure" experiment does not work for many situations. It is difficult to examine, for example, the effects of different types of peers on adolescents by the researcher changing the nature of the peer group for students. It is difficult not only because there are ethical issues, but also because it is virtually impossible to have that much control. So we use observational methods. In such cases the replicable methods become a procedure for obtaining data on peer groups and adolescent changes observed over time, such as in the work of the Jessors (Jessor, Graves, Hanson, & Jessor, 1968).

At the top of the pyramid are the disciplines that seek to develop more comprehensive statements, such as worldviews. Philosophy, for example, wrestles with the implications of quantum physics that depart from a pure mechanistic causation. Theology seeks to understand and express how facts from science, seen as revelatory of the world God created, are related to Biblical revelation relevant to the same facts. So both philosophy and theology are concerned with what the disciplines in the science pyramid conclude.

Perhaps the relationships of the disciplines at the top of the pyramid to those toward the bottom can be explored by noting the impact of science models on worldviews. In the seventeenth and eighteenth centuries physics found many mechanistic principles, and these resulted in engineering applications that were striking to the people of those times. One such engineering marvel from basic physics was the clock. When first introduced, it was a magnificently impressive device. Nothing that people created had ever before run under its own power and yet could be understood in detail. It impacted worldviews, giving the deistic theology that God created a universe just like a clock, wound it up and started it, and then let it run (Boorstin, 1983, p. 71).

We can expect contemporary science to also impact worldviews, and vice versa. This mutual impact is at the heart of integration when cross-discipline impact is based on dialogue between the disciplines.

PHILOSOPHY AND PSYCHOLOGY
AS THE BASIS OF SCIENCE

The classical pyramid presented earlier has several major limitations. One important limitation is that it ignores that physics itself is not quite the base of the pyramid. Instead, it rests upon assumptions regarding the nature of reality and our relationship to it. Science as commonly practiced implicitly assumes that our experiences show us reality, a reality that was the same in the past as it is now. That is the basis for using light from stars so distant that it shows what those stars were like billions of years ago. In addition, all engineering assumes that the principles established today will be the same tomorrow. The assumptions underlying even physics—such as the consistency of the world—are not addressed by physics. Instead, they need to be justified by philosophy and theology.

The classical science just described can be argued to be based upon two major theological points. First, Judeo–Christian–Islamic theology notes that "God is the same yesterday, today, and tomorrow" (Hebrews 13:8). This provides a worldview that expects to find a universe that is the same yesterday, today, and tomorrow. The universe has basic, unchanging characteristics from one day to the next. Without such a worldview, science is not reasonable. We would have no basis to check for replicable facts.

A second major theological point supporting classical science is the role of people in relationship to the world. The Bible is clear that we are given dominion over the world (Genesis 1:28). This is illustrated in Genesis when God brings all the creatures to be named by people. It means that while we do not have ownership, we do have control. Having control means we are responsible for how we use that control. Control means that we can change things, and that is a necessary assumption for the experiment to be a basis for understanding reality. Since we have dominion over the world, we also need to know that world in-depth in order to make the right decisions in carrying out the responsibility that goes with that dominion. Thus, this theological worldview presses us toward science. If science did not exist, these elements of Christian theology would require us to invent it. Exhibit 2.3 gives an example of a society without these theological understandings.

Exhibit 2.3
An Anti-Science Theology

In reading the *Iliad* (Homer, 700 B.C./1990), the descriptions of the Greek gods and goddesses give the Greeks' theological worldview. They viewed the gods as anything but "steadfast." The Greek gods were certainly active in the world. Events every day were attributed to the action of the gods. Nowhere is this more obvious than in Homer's descriptions of battles.

In a battle all soldiers wanted powerful gods on their side. So they made sacrifices and promises to assure that. But what happened on a battlefield? The god you trust may help you or may, in the midst of battle, leave you to your fate. Homer notes that Zeus had the Trojans and Hector attack the Achaians at their beached ships. Then "he left them . . . to endure fighting without respite" while Zeus "turned his eyes shining far away" (Homer, 700 B.C./1990, p. 148). There was no way you could predict the gods' actions, and so who would ever try?

Commentary: There can be no basis for science when events of the past, present, and future depend on capricious deities. Greek philosophers have been important in the history of the Western world and science. However, those philosophers took the gods less seriously than Homer's characters—much less seriously.

Added to the notion of control, although not necessary as a basis for science, are the Biblical instructions that we serve others. It can be suggested that dominion and serving others leads to an active engineering program being developed from and requiring a strong science. The results are seen, for example, in the development of agricultural science. Christian farmers often see themselves in the ministry of feeding the hungry, and they encourage and use the latest research they know. This research has led to the "green revolution" of the twentieth century that allowed us to feed so many people.

Philosophy also has a role in providing a foundation to undergird the pyramid, and that is in analyzing how and when we can know reality. Most scientists have assumed that our senses give us reasonably accurate information, but philosophy has the obligation to explore whether this is so. Are our senses reporting on reality and is that report a faithful one? The Greek philosophers had varied opinions on this question, and it has been an issue of primary importance during the last century.

The crucial current philosophical debate centers on whether we can "know," truly know with 100-percent certainty. Descartes (1701/1990) asked this question. He, as most, noted that mathematics was a system that, when granting its assumptions, could give proofs with 100-percent certainty. But could anything else?

Descartes decided to accept only that for which no doubt could be raised. He considered much, and found that he could doubt much. Indeed, he asked if there was anything he could not doubt. Exhibit 2.4 illustrates that a person can indeed, when his or her mind is set to it, doubt much.

EXHIBIT 2.4
I Know I Exist, but Do You?

An alternative worldview that is logically consistent with my experience is that only I exist. You are, in this alternate worldview, a figment of my imagination. I would apologize for thus excluding you from existence, but that would imply you are real.

Perhaps I am God and have invented not only you but also this whole universe to pass the time.

Perhaps I am in a deep psychosis and you are a part of that psychosis.

Perhaps you are an imaginary playmate from my childhood that I have convinced myself is real.

Perhaps I am the subject in a master experiment and you are a robot programmed to help create the environment that is desired. After you leave me or put down this book, you are put on "inactive status" until the time comes again for you to be part of my environment or to pick up this book again. The fact that you report your personal existence as real is not crucial; you may just be programmed with such communications to be part of a consistent environment.

Or perhaps I am like the lead character in the 1998 movie, *The Truman Show*. You are an actor taught to act your part in building "my world."

Commentary: For these theories, there is no evidence that could falsify them. However, unless they can be eliminated, I cannot conclusively prove you exist. I, however, find it more interesting to accept your existence (and that of the universe) as a working assumption—at least the existence of those who read this book.

Descartes's conclusion is in his widely quoted Latin phrase, "Cogito, ergo sum" (Descartes, 1701/1990, pp. 275–276), which translates as "I think, therefore I am." The thinking refers to the doubting, for the one thing that Descartes found he could not doubt was that doubting occurred. The doubting implied that there was something doing the doubting. However, Descartes was an optimist by adding the "I," for that is virtually void of meaning. We know nothing of the "I" from the act of doubting. That is why I like to rephrase the translation of the Latin without a subject: "Thinking, therefore being." Indeed, the implication that "something" exists other than doubting is difficult to prove, since it assumes a definition of existence.

The average person and Descartes have this in common: Neither have taken his or her doubting of the existence of everything else too seriously. In fact, Descartes only devoted two pages to this argument. Then he gave only the next two pages to build a foundation that went beyond that argument to give God and the natural world existence. Given the extent of Descartes's writing, he took this argument less seriously than we do. In addition, he, as we, continued to live a normal life, interacting with people, and so forth. Descartes was able to find philosophical justification for doing so by building a "foundation" for reality based in part in his theology.

Philosophers have taken "cogito, ergo sum" seriously, but not Descartes's foundation. And the "postmodern" era can be identified as the era when philosophers have given up—after searching for several hundred years—on finding any *conclusive* foundation on which to build a philosophy of knowledge. Every foundation tried so far seems to give way to the possibility of being doubted.

What does this have to do with Christians? Has not God broken through to them with the truth? Since Christians believe God created the world and people, they believe in that reality. So why do we need philosophy at all?

Yes, Christians do believe that. However, those beliefs do not come from a vacuum. Let's consider two examples. First, consider a Christian who has a conversion experience. To attribute that to God and to Jesus requires that he or she first know about God and Jesus (that is why missionaries are deemed important). I know of no case in which a conversion to Christ happened without God laying the groundwork through Christians or the Bible carrying the message to them at some point in their lives.

A second example for why some philosophy precedes theology are the Biblical beliefs underlying faith. We believe because of what the Bible tells us. However, note that such Biblical belief is based on the belief that the Bible is true. We read scriptures of other faiths but do not attribute the same truth value to them, even though those scriptures claim to be true and millions of people say they are true. What is the basis for our acceptance of the truth of the Bible rather than some other Scriptures or no Scriptures at all? For most of us it is a combination of other's and our own convictions that lead us to believe the Biblical message is true. So even our faith needs a foundation on which to base our conclusion that Biblical Christianity is true (this is a topic addressed in depth in philosophy of religion and theology books, such as C. Brown, 1968).

Descartes and philosophy have assumed a model of absolute proof of reality that relies solely on logic. It means that the rational decision maker in this area—and by extension in other areas, including both science and theology—considers only the evidence for the validity of the argument in total absence of reference to any other data or considerations. But is this a rational decision maker?

The discipline that has been studying human decision making for almost a century is that of psychology. It is my contention that the model of rational decision making underlying Descartes's logic and that of many postmodernists has some illogical elements and so is fundamentally flawed; in other words, we can seriously doubt conclusions based on "cogito, ergo sum" because the assumptions underlying the method leading to the conclusions are flawed.

There are models, supported by psychology and logic, that produce a different conclusion. They date back at least to Pascal (1670/1990), and lead to a proposal that provides a basis for knowledge of both science and religion. Typical of these are utility models, such as those known in social psychology as "reasoned action" models (Ajzen & Fishbein, 1980; Ajzen, 1988; Triandis, 1971). In such cases the long-term consequences of a decision are part of the decision-making model. No decision reached without taking these into account can be termed rational. In fact, Damasio (1994) notes that certain cases of brain damage produce illogical behavior because the person no longer takes into account the long-term impact of his or her decisions. Does this mean that philosophers and theologians who reach decisions within their areas without considering long-term consequences are wrong? That is a question that needs considerable attention before we draw far-reaching conclusions from "cogito, ergo sum," but it does seem that philosophical conclusions based solely on this quote resemble illogical decision making. (I reject the alternative that they are brain damaged.)

Because of the centrality of human decision making not only to science and religion but also to the philosophy of knowledge, psychology is a base that underlies all these areas. Thus, scientific psychology has a dual role to play: its usual one as the science between biology and sociology and its new role in analyzing the basis of human knowledge, which is the foundation for physics and the rest of the pyramid.

PSYCHOLOGY'S ODD RELATIONSHIP
WITH PHILOSOPHY

In the last section I concluded that psychology of knowledge is critical to understanding philosophy of knowledge. This is not, of course, a widely held view in the sense that philosophers are quoting the latest psychological research. Indeed, given the age of psychology, the absence of debate on psychology's role in knowledge raises the question of why. While cognitive and social psychologists have been developing knowledge essential to the knowledge task, why have philosophers (and psychologists) been so ignorant of it?

I have suggested (Gorsuch, 1988) that the journey of psychology in the past century and its avoidance of issues included in this book is a function of its history in establishing itself as a "scientific discipline." The short form of this argument is that psychology and philosophy were fused before World War I. This is shown by a major figure of that era, William James. He is well known as both a philosopher and a psychologist. Indeed, before psychology departments were formed, the work of psychology was done by philosophers in philosophy departments.

As psychological method began and a group of people became known as psychologists, they moved out of philosophy departments and formed separately departments of psychology. To do so, they had to defend this action to university administrations. In addition, they had to explain to students how this new discipline differed from philosophy.

The early psychologists did not differ from philosophy as much as we might think. The "introspective" program of research was a refinement of self-observation, such as Descartes did to show how much could be doubted. It could have been difficult to explain why a separate program was needed for it.

The behaviorism revolution in psychology was successful because it answered the need for a psychology that was clearly not philosophy. It rejected anything resembling philosophical methods or topics, which included theology as well. Only if it were pure behavior could the psychologist be assured that it would not be mistaken for philosophy. That definition of and approach to psychology was needed by the first generation of psychologists to "win their spurs" among the scientists. And like most paradigms, they taught it—perhaps more by example than by word—to the next generation of psychologists. So it continued to the next generation, through World War II.

The first generations of psychologists did their work well in distinguishing psychology from philosophy. After World War II it was accepted that psychology was, if not quite a "real" science to "hard-liners," at least independent of philosophy and established as a "social" or "behavioral" science. The first post–World War II generation had lingering habits because their graduate school professors were still in the world of "we don't do anything that could be confused with philosophy because we're a science!"

For the next generation, in the 1960s, there was no longer the need to distinguish psychology from philosophy. Now topics such as cognition and religion could be reopened, but not as philosophy. Instead, the topics were approached from a science of psychology with methods that had several generations of development. This gave rise, almost simultaneously, to cognitive psychology and psychology of religion.

It takes time for a discipline to build up a worthwhile base of data and theories. Nevertheless, relevant areas of psychology have now had such time. Psychology can be relevant for philosophy, and spirituality can be relevant for psychology.

SPIRITUALITY DISCIPLINES AND TRUTH

The disciplines most associated with spirituality are nonscientific, such as philosophy and theology. They are more closely associated with the humanities, such as history and biography. But how do these disciplines find "truth"?

In twentieth-century philosophies, a discipline could only find truth if it could present logical and positive evidence for hypotheses that were falsifiable. The terms "positive" and "falsifiable" were crucial. The former meant that one needed to go beyond thought and logic; clear evidence needed to be documented. The latter meant that evidence was truly evidence only if the study could have come out some other way.

The twentieth-century logical positivists, arguing from the need for positive evidence about falsifiable hypotheses, saw only science as meeting the criteria for truth. What, then, of the humanities? They just provided expressions of attitudes or values. Indeed, the heart of the humanities was in the stories told, and they did not need to be real to be meaningful. This last point can be seen in fiction that impacted people's views of the world and what it should be like. Skinner's (1976) *Walden Two* is a good example. It was written to showcase what Skinner thought a truly scientific behaviorism could offer the world. Of course, it was just a story. The real basis of truth was in science.

The end of the twentieth century shifted the view of science. That shift was spurred by Kuhn's (1970) *The Structure of Scientific Revolutions*, in which Kuhn argued that scientific truth was a function of paradigms. Paradigms were the general assumptions and perspectives that dominated a scientific field until a revolution appeared that radically changed the paradigm. These paradigm shifts reworked the data into new configurations and generated new theoretical positions.

The notion of paradigms has been used with spiritualities as well. It has been used to suggest that different religions are just different paradigms, as if that made them all equal. But there is little in the use of paradigms describing science to imply that all theories or paradigms are equal. Neither is there support for the position that all sciences are just alternative paradigms—or stories—and so have the same truth value as spiritualities. Instead, within this project scientific paradigms must meet scientific criteria and spirituality paradigms must meet spiritual criteria.

Personal Integration and Idiographic Truth

Psychology is a part of the scientific disciplines and also has a role with philosophy and theology. That covers what we termed "professional integration," which, since people do the science, also includes some personal integration. But we have also noted that people live more than in their professions and that ethics, theology, and psychology all should speak to that life, giving personal integration. How then do we relate such disciplines to personal integration?

The disciplines involved are those in which we express ourselves as humanity, and not just as scientists. The term "human" in the previous sentence is deliberate, for it is my contention that the humanities are important disciplines to our everyday—our existential—situations. We live not by "ologies" alone. Individual decisions that we make differ from decisions as a professional. In individual situations we bring, for example, our histories, a very personal history for each of us. Each of these histories is unique.

Uniqueness underlies the distinction between "nomothetic" and "idiographic." **Nomothetic is concerned with that which can be generalized, such as basic principles. Idiographic is concerned with that which is unique (and therefore not generalizable).** The purposes and procedures of science are nomothetic. Science seeks the basic principles that govern a particular situation each and every time that the situation arises. The individual case is, hopefully, predictable as a generalization from all relevant nomothetic principles, but the purpose is nomothetic. Of course, then, the procedures are oriented to produce nomothetic knowledge. This is found in that multiple scientists produce the same basic results from the same procedures. Variations in those outcomes, which would reflect idiographic influences, are relegated to error (which is what they are from a nomothetic viewpoint).

Nevertheless, every one of us lives an idiographic life. Each event is unique in the sense that it never happens again in exactly the same way. As a Greek philosopher said, "You cannot step in the same stream twice." The time between step 1 and step 2 is sufficient for leaves to fall into it, for different particles of water to be where you are stepping, and so forth, and that makes it a different stream. Indeed, even the first step itself changes the stream sufficiently so that it could be said to not be the same stream (if this sounds a little odd—for do we not call the Mississippi the Mississippi no matter who steps in it?— just chalk it up to philosophical attempts to be very precise!). In the same way, no person experiences exactly the same event twice.

An idiographic event may, for better or worse, shift someone's life into a radically different direction. When chairing our admissions committee, I point out that inviting a student to study in our school is a unique event in that person's life. Our decision will change that life radically, particularly when we are the only school to which he or she applies. Our one decision changes many things for the rest of that student's life, including his or her income, where he or she lives, how he or she is perceived by others, what he or she will probably die of, his or her relationship to the Church, and, if single, who he or she will marry. The one decision is a cusp; after that decision, everything changes. A culture can also have a cusp event that changes it dramatically. Columbus's discovery of the "New World" was a cusp, particularly for the Americas. The death of Jesus was a cusp that changed the world.

Each of us—in the roles of person, scientist, scholar, and so on—

approaches even the most nomothetic from our own idiographic perspective. This is recognized in studying the Bible: Johnson (1983), for example, emphasizes how our unique histories and personalities affect interpreting scripture, and that they should. In like manner, scientists approach their disciplines from their own idiographic perspectives (Kuhn, 1970, gives some illustrations of this).

While we may theorize and even dream in a nomothetic world, we never live in it. We live in very idiographic worlds, each one with its own history. Our memories are filled with idiographic, unique events, and these events give us major parts of our identity.

The disciplines that are most linked to the idiographic events of life are in the arts and humanities. They express our situations—including spiritual ones—in ways that communicate beyond the formal, logical exposition of nomothetic science. The arts themselves are expressions of our idiographic selves, and we resonate with art that "strikes the right cord" with us. In fact, is it not a common experience to feel more in touch with ultimate reality through arts and humanities than through sciences?

The idiographic is also central in our professional and personal lives because of the nature of "understanding and insight." While nomothetically we support the theory that even the insights that we have follow nomothetic principles, how the insights happen is still idiographic to each of us. Exhibit 2.5 is an illustration of a movie helping bring closure for me to the issue of how a Christian may be able to be a chaplain or psychologist in war. It is more theology than psychology, but it might provide a base for a clinical psychologist called to work with a veteran or army.

EXHIBIT 2.5
The Chaplain's or Psychologist's Role with Soldiers

One problem for me has been how to help someone serving in the military in times of war. I know that war is a total breakdown of civilization, and that the odds of my nation being right are not 100 percent. The other side could be right, so what are we to do? Do we need to decide ourselves whether each fight is a "just" war and support only the soldiers fighting on the "just" side? I know too much social psychology and too much history. Almost all of us would pick our own nation's side as the just one no matter which nation we were born in (unless we wanted to prove that we are stubbornly independent; then we support the side none of our people support!).

My resolution of this vexing problem came from viewing the 1986 movie

The Mission. The story is of several Catholic missionaries working with a tribe in South America when, due to complex European politics, the tribe is reallocated from the Spanish to the Portuguese. The Portuguese move in to enslave the tribe. The missionaries respond to this threat as each feels called by the Spirit. One takes up a gun to help the tribe defend themselves and another celebrates communion as pacifist protest. Both die without affecting the outcome, as do most of the people of that tribe. However, soldiers on the other side die also. Like the natives, they probably thought their cause was right. How can we hope to know who is right?

Commentary: I doubt if you received any major insights from this story, and you probably would not from renting the movie. One of the points here is that these personal experiences are personal.

What of the actions of the missionaries in *The Mission*? The question of who was right concerned me. "But," the idea suddenly occurred, "may not all of them be right?" Psychologically I could say that they each had their own history, and their choices were probably outgrowths of those idiographic histories. However, theologically God does call different people to different tasks, even in the same setting. One missionary may well have been called to take up a gun while another was called to pacific resistance. We must help people to be open to their own calls.

This led to another insight: God is with the soldiers on both sides regardless of who is right or wrong. We need, as ministers and psychologists, to help the soldiers live through and, hopefully, grow from that experience. They have little choice as to which army they serve. So being concerned about whether it is a just war could be our agenda, but it is not the agenda of the soldiers we serve as psychologists or chaplains. God is in the foxhole on both sides. It doesn't matter which side we are on when it comes to helping the soldier. (In our role as citizens we each do need to help our nation make the right decisions, of course. Then our integration is with both ethics and the social psychology of conflict management, as in Chapter 6.)

As B. Strossberg (e-mail, 3 January 2002) has noted, our discussion of disciplines applies to the study of art and literature. Even as science uses replicable events to build into a conceptual framework, the humanities take our idiographic events and build them into a conceptual framework. That is why the top of the pyramid contains theology, not religion. Theology is the discipline addressing religion.

For us in psychology the most important disciplines of the humanities are probably literature and history. Literature is concerned with the ebb and flow of humans in their contexts. Biography obviously fits into that category, but so does good fiction, as it plays out the lives of people in their unique situations. Movies are an expression of the same but in another medium. These are the ways in which an individual, idiographic life is portrayed.

History is important for understanding the unique events that are background to present interactions, whether of professionals dialoging over what should be done next, politicians considering their choices, or Christians mediating between warring parties. A profession is open to or rejecting of possible directions of movement depending on where they have been in the past. Our discussion has noted the impact of psychology coming out of philosophy on the possibility of integration. How much different would our current position be if the founders of psychology had come from history instead?

Applied disciplines are combinations of the nomothetic and idiographic. While the nomothetic provides orientation to, for example, counseling a couple, the calling of the psychologist who works with that couple is to adapt and fit the nomothetic into the unique history of that couple.

The following list contains a pyramid for idiographic understanding, a pyramid of the humanities (Gorsuch, 2002). The foundation is that of our personal experience, which is of great importance to us. There is nothing so convincing of the existence of God as carrying on a conversation with God. From our own experience and that of others come the other humanities:

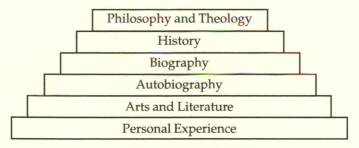

Literature is represented in manifestations that include biography and fiction, prose and poetry. From the events recorded in many individual lives comes history, the recording and understanding of people in groups. At the top again are philosophy and theology for the same reason they were at the top of the science pyramid: They attempt to "pull it all together" and make sense of it.

The addition of the pyramid of humanities and noting that the humanities are concerned with idiographic truth (rather than science's nomothetic) provides a place of respect for some areas that are left out of typical psychology (Vande Kemp, 1996, 1998). That part of a phenomenological analysis that does not meet the criterion for science does not mean it is false or worthless. What it does mean is that it may fall into the more idiographic areas of experience, such as art, literature, and the humanities in general.

But is only science objective? Given our earlier definition—agreement among raters using the same definition—the answer is "no." An idiographic discipline such as history looks for rater agreement not by replication (science) but by checking for consistency of reports across records or memories.

One could do personal integration through active consideration of the several disciplines as they apply in the pyramid of the humanities. However, personal integration as a psychologist requires more, for it requires blending across both pyramids. One must be able to bring our nomothetic knowledge as psychologists into touch with our personal experience, expression in the arts, and relevant parts of the humanities. We move toward personal and professional integration when we ask, for example, what our history has to teach us about our current situation, or when we ask how our psychology informs what is more and less likely to occur, or how our theology shapes our ethics in this situation.

Note that it is impossible for anyone to be an expert in more than one's own discipline due to the complexity of all the modern disciplines. Perhaps we can at least be open to input from others in these disciplines, and consciously seek to draw from them. Perhaps here in the United States we need to recognize the value of the greater focus on breath and liberal arts found in Europe.

What we must be careful to do is to realize that each discipline has its role and no discipline should usurp the other. Psychologists are great at researching nomothetic principles, but few could write a good biography. Moreover, interviewing three people and writing up their stories is, of course, appropriate for journalists and biographers, but nothing about a philosopher's, sociologist's, or psychologist's training prepares them for such a role. Reading what the journalist or biographer has found and using that to inform one's psychology or theology is a step toward personal integration. The integration task is making the sciences (which include psychology) and humanities (which include the disciplines concerned with spirituality) the warp and woof in the fabric of our lives.

A CONCLUDING NOTE

The earlier discussion of science stressed that nothing is accepted until it is replicated by other scientists in their own experiences. This means science's truth is ultimately based in personal experience, just as is the humanities'.

EXERCISE

Read a good short story. Then look through your psychology and ethics texts and find examples of the nomothetic principles underlying that story. Play some "what if" games working from the psychology principles to develop alternative directions that might have been taken. How would you theologically evaluate those alternative directions?

This will seem very strange. As with any new endeavor, it takes multiple tries to develop enough expertise for conscious integration to come naturally.

PART II

INTERDISCIPLINARY COMMENTARY

In the preceding chapters we have considered the relationships among the disciplines concerned with integration, particularly psychology and spirituality. These lay the basis for integration. Integration can be divided into two major types (see Chapter 1). The first type, Interdisciplinary Commentary, is where one discipline makes suggestions for another. This differs from the first two chapters since those involved general critiques of multiple disciplines. Chapters 3 and 4 attempt Interdisciplinary Commentary by exploring some issues that spirituality such as Christianity raises for sciences such as psychology (Chapter 3), and by exploring some issues that sciences such as psychology raise for spirituality (Chapter 4). These critiques remind us that neither spirituality nor science dictates to the other, but that each might learn more about its own tasks by hearing what the other has to say.

Spirituality: On the Limits of Science (Psychology)

Given the nature of the science of psychology as described so far, it is appropriate to explore what spirituality may see as issues to raise with science, particularly on the limits of science. The first issue to be discussed is modes of knowledge. While science is certainly a major mode for knowledge, Chapter 2 already suggests that the humanities may look upon knowledge somewhat differently, and that is explored as the first topic of this chapter.

Since spirituality involves ethics, spiritual persons usually object to the complete determinism associated with the classical science approach to psychology. Moreover, they wish to note that sciences generally assume a neutral universe, avoiding terms such as good and bad, and so perhaps they "have blinders on" when the problem of evil arises. Can and does psychology recognize evil or is that what spirituality needs to add?

Given the breath of spirituality, the points discussed here are samples of the topics that could be included. Even an entire book would be insufficient to cover this area fully. Moreover, each topic could be approached from several different spiritualities, worldviews, or theologies. This chapter shall approach topics both from spirituality in general and from Christianity in particular.

Note that some of the areas here are included because they immediately come to mind. After the discussion, you may decide if they are weak or strong commentary.

MODES FOR ACQUIRING KNOWLEDGE

Sciences assume that all knowledge comes through the physical senses. This includes the senses as augmented by scientific instruments. If we cannot see, touch, or hear a phenomena—and the "we" means replicate that phenomena—then it is outside the realm of scientific knowledge. Many scientists seem to feel that science is the only mode by which knowledge becomes available to us, although science was shown in Chapter 2 to be limited to nomothetic truth. Spirituality suggests that we, as people, have other approaches to knowledge. How do these differ from science and what might they add?

"Natural theology," the first mode discussed here, is a spirituality mode of knowledge that uses science but understands it through the lens of spirituality. It notes that natural philosophy and theology are the study of natural phenomena (via science) to see what it tells us about, for example, the nature of God. While natural theology is helpful, is such use of science reductionistic and therefore handicapped in integrating with spirituality?

For integration, modes of finding knowledge more independent of science than natural theology are useful in addition to science. These include personal experience and history. While not all types of spirituality would consider the same materials to be sacred, revelation is another major source for truth within many traditions.

Modes of knowledge outside of science, spirituality suggests, need to be considered as limits on science in the sense that spirituality goes where science has difficulties. Do they also allow possibilities of spiritual knowledge on issues relevant to psychology beyond the bounds of science; if so, what may that look like?

Natural Theology

Natural theology is drawing conclusions relevant to spirituality from nature, particularly for ethics in the sense of moving from "is" to "ought." So a "fact of nature" shows not only what is but what should be. It has a long history. For example, Augustine left the Manichian religious group because their teachings did not agree with the scientific findings regarding astronomy. In his case, natural theology took precedence over one sect's teachings, although he also chided the secular astronomers for their lack of respect for God's establishing the observed regularities (see Augustine, 400/1990, pp. 34–39, as an early example of integrating spirituality and science).

Natural theology asks what the implications are of scientific findings for understanding the natural order and where we fit within it.

Obviously, this is aligned in Christianity with the concept of God the creator. Since God created the world, scientific findings are findings regarding God's will. No physical law exists but that God established it.

For example, we do natural theology when we decide, based on the research data, to take 400 IUs of vitamin E every day. The research has shown that taking this supplement decreases free radicals, strengthens the immune system, and decreases the deposit on blood vessel walls, all of which reduce the likelihood of disease (e.g., Raloff, 1988). This is natural theology because it is based in science that guides behavior with the assumption that good health is best. Vitamin E, the supplement, is theologically good because the research shows that God made us needing this vitamin (at least for long life in our current environment, an environment which is not exactly the Garden of Eden).

From a natural theology perspective, psychology tells us much about how God created us to live. It can be examined for the "vitamins" that reduce stress and its effects. It can be examined for what parenting practices are most likely to help children grow to be ethical adults, or to grow to meet the ideals of a particular religious group. Psychological research can be seen as finding the best ways to live to maximize our spirituality. In this manner, psychology finds God's will for people in general.

"But," persons concerned with spirituality ask, "are all God's acts researchable by science and so part of natural theology?" In Christianity there are several reasons to feel that such is not the case. The first is the problem of our limited minds being able to understand a complex being such as God just as we would physics or some other area of science. Exhibit 3.1 gives an illustration of how a finding in developmental psychology illustrates the limits of our understanding and so handicaps natural theology's understandings, and thus limits science's potential contributions to spirituality.

EXHIBIT 3.1
Does God Reason at a Higher Stage Than We?

From McDougall (1908) through Peck and Havinghurst (1960), Kohlberg (1969), and Darley, Glucksberg, and Kinchla (1988), psychologists have recorded stages of reasoning that children pass through as they grow. The earliest stage involves some comprehension but almost no reasoning as we would recognize it; it is typical of preschool children. The next stage has reasoning following a logic taking very concrete steps. Arithmetic is understood. This concrete logic is used to determine, for example, if the cookies are worth the risk of being caught. As adults we use a higher stage, formal operations, which involves abstract reasoning, including that of higher mathematics. These stages affect scientific, mathematical, ethical, and other reasoning.

Children asked why a person should help a drowning child will, at the concrete operations stage, give an answer that is based on what happens immediately to them. At the abstract reasoning stage, an answer about the value of life is more typical (Bull, 1969).

What happens if an explanation is given to a child in a more adult rationale than the child is capable of handling? The child interprets it to a level that is understandable. If one has a calculus problem but knows only algebra, then the best solution using algebra is tried. The "higher stage" of knowing calculus incorporates algebra and is able to use them both appropriately.

If a child at the lower stage is told that "it is good to save a drowning child's life because each person is valuable," they are likely to repeat it back as "saving a child's life is good because you may get something valuable." The former is an abstract principle whereas the latter is a concrete form of reasoning.

Moreover, if you pressed them, "What if there were no valuable reward. Should you save the child's life?" they might say, "If you want to." If you respond, "And if you don't feel like it?" they might reply, "That's OK. Don't do it." This shows that they did not understand the abstract principle mentioned by the adult.

If a child is presented with a rationale that is at a higher stage, the child rewrites it down to a level that child can understand. Venable and Gorsuch (1999) gave spiritual motivation rationales that were either intrinsic or extrinsic to children. The latter looks for external rewards to be spiritual; the former is spiritual for the sake of spirituality itself. As hypothesized, the intrinsic children understood extrinsic arguments as evidenced by reproducing them correctly. But the extrinsic child did not understand intrinsic arguments, as evidenced by their inability to reproduce them.

Consider the human dilemma of understanding God. It can be argued that God's thinking is beyond our thinking. In that case, there should be rationales that we understand poorly. Or, perhaps even more dangerous, we rewrite God's rationale to our lower level of thinking.

Commentary: Any scientific theory in a complex area that we can reason out has probably rewritten the rationale from God's higher stage to our own. That is part of science's purpose, to make the world understandable to our human minds. Being rewritten, we are not surprised by an occasional inconsistency.

Any systematic theology that has a rationale for everything—with nothing of mystery—has probably rewritten the rationale from God's higher stage to our own. That is part of theology's purpose, to make it understandable to our human minds. Being rewritten, we are not surprised by an occasional inconsistency.

A little humility is in order for both the theologian and scientist.

Exhibit 3.1 points to the limits of what we can expect. As Templeton (1995) has said, "Only arrogance would lead others to assert that what they cannot comprehend cannot exist" (p. 14). However, this should never mean we stop trying to understand, for any increase in understanding the basic nature of the universe is helpful to spirituality. Nor does it mean that we can argue from ignorance: "If we don't understand it, then it must be true." For the more likely alternative explanation is that we have not studied sufficiently or we are just not up to it (and someone else may be).

Arguing from science's findings of "what is" to "that must be God's way" is always limited by our narrow view. For example, observation consistently finds that major sections of our world exist on a "nothing is certain except death by being eaten" basis, which I sometimes call the "death by dinner" principle. Most species of fish live by eating other fish. Just check the mouths of any fish, such as bass and muskellunge: They have quite formidable teeth, made only for attack on other fish.

Note that "death by dinner" is designed into these creatures. For many fish no other food has been found to keep them alive except live smaller fish. And the fish that has the smaller fish as dinner becomes dinner for a large fish. So God wanted a "fish eat fish" world. The lion cannot lie down with the lamb unless either the lion's teeth are pulled or the lion's appetite is assuaged by the death of creatures other than the lamb. That's an accurate description of the world.

For most spiritualities, natural theology is not taken to the place that the last paragraph would suggest. Spiritualities would agree that giving of one's life so that another lives is worthwhile, although the "death by dinner" fish may not see it that way. And God is seen as wanting something different for us, and possibly for other creatures as well. It is interesting that people have invented meat substitutes so "the lamb can lie down with the lion." Perhaps that's a task God has given us. Nothing in science (which includes psychology) can help us answer a question of what tasks God has given us, but spirituality can.

What are some approaches spirituality may take toward the "death by dinner" facts? In addition to the suggestion that the purpose of people may be to reduce this, there are several viable explanations. Templeton (1995) suggests that suffering in this manner may be to strengthen us spiritually. But perhaps it is a "death by dinner" world to prevent suffering. "Death by dinner" is swift, and so is suffering writ small; death prolonged by medicine that neither cures the illness nor controls the pain is suffering writ large.

Reductionism

Reductionism refers to reducing a more complex phenomenon to simpler, underlying principles, principles that may bear little resemblance to what the phenomenon may appear to be. An inherent problem of some scientific approaches to spiritual issues has arisen because of reductionistic thinking.

Freud is a good example of reductionists when spirituality is considered. In the preface to *The Future of an Illusion*, Freud (1927/1964) clearly states that religion—which includes all spirituality with a "higher power"—is obviously wrong. This is stated as an assumption, and no rationale is given. If you assume spirituality is wrong, your only option is to identify something else that causes it than what the spirituality claims causes it. A concept assumed false must be explained away, and that is what Freud tries to do. This, of course, has made integration of Freudian psychology and spirituality difficult (Sorenson, 1994a, 1994b).

From a spirituality view, Freud has missed the whole debate. He has assumed spirituality must be reduced; he neither reasoned nor found by research that it must be. Because of the assumption, the rest of the argument is poor science; it is nonfalsifiable and no test of any hypothesis. Moreover, it is not an integration discussion because he allows no discussion with the "obviously false" spirituality.

Cattell (e.g., Cattell & Child, 1975) makes the same assumption as Freud. Since spiritualities are "just superstition"—a comment RBC often made in private conversation and in Beyondism (Cattell, 1987)—it must come from extrinsic motivations, regardless of what the person considers its source. Hence, religion is based, for RBC, in more basic drives, such as fear and paternalism. His motivational research found the expected correlations of these drives with religiousness. This can be expanded to spiritual experiences of any kind.

Natural theology is certainly useful and psychology provides interesting data, but it becomes theology only when integrated with spirituality. Denying the possibility of spirituality leads solely to reductionism. Neither Freud nor RBC dealt with integration because they were closed to the possibility of spirituality.

Can Natural Theology Use Science Research for God's Individual Acts?

Science can find God's steadfast acts, such as the ways of the natural world. There is considerable debate about how God might act outside of the natural laws of science (Russell, Murphy, & Peacocke, 1995, go into this in detail; Russell, 1995, has a basic overview).

What of applying research methods to topics such as prayer? Prayer is asking for an individual act of God, an act not covered in the natural laws (which show God's habitual, consistent way of acting). Would people who are prayed for have a noticeably better recovery than those not prayed for?

Few Christians would base their belief in God or in the power of prayer in such studies. There are several reasons for this (Gorsuch, 2002). One is that it is almost impossible to have a true control group; that is, a group that is not being prayed for. The control's own family may be praying for them, as well as their minister and other Christians. In addition, they would be included in thousands if not millions of "generic" prayers ("Lord, help those who are sick this day"). While the sheer volume of prayers is important in some religions, that is not the case in those studies that assume a Christian God. In neither scripture nor church tradition is the number of prayers crucial.

We do not know how God uses our prayers, but there is no theological basis for suggesting that God sees the prayers of the researchers as more important than the other prayers, or that God decides to act based on counts of the number of people praying. So why should the prayers of the researchers make any difference when the controls are also being prayed for? God does not play favorites and so cure only people the researchers pray for. Neither does God cure people because of the greater number of prayers because of the researchers.

Another theological problem is that the prayer research studies assume that better health and longer life is God's answer to those prayers. Many Christians would suggest that quality of life in the faith is the important issue, not long life. A God who let his own son be killed at thirty-three years of age does not seem caught up in a "life at any price" spiritually. And Paul, in prison just before his death, "had learned to depend on God to judge what his true needs were and how they were to be met" (Brown, 1985, p. 189). Hence, praying "Your will be done, O Lord" for some might lead to a quicker death. Or it may mean the death occurs at the appropriate time to challenge a family member to deeper spirituality. These would be counted as outcomes against prayer in research studies "testing prayer," but would be theologically sound answers to the prayers.

There is a basic problem in science's methods for investigating God's individual activities in the world. Science can and does, from a Christian view, identify how God continually and steadfastly operates time after time. These acts of God are replicable, because they occur consistently time after time. The problem with investigating God's individual acts, such as in prayer research, is that the act is for an individual idiographic (as defined in Chapter 2) event.

Christianity holds that God operates on an idiographic, individual level as well as on the level of nomothetic law. We call such actions "miracles" if they are spectacular and seen through the eye of faith. But they cannot be confirmed or refuted by science, being on the idiographic level.

Why can science neither confirm nor refute an individual act of God? Because, as noted in Chapter 2, the method of science is replication. If it replicates, then a scientific conclusion can be drawn. If it does not replicate, then no scientific conclusion can be drawn. By definition, God's individual acts do not replicate. So science can never identify them even if they happen a dozen times a day in every scientist's life.

What happens in science when a result is found that does not replicate? It is considered a fluke and ignored. If it is published, it generally stops being cited, as people cannot replicate it (recall Exhibit 2.2 on cold fusion). Often it is not even published, but just put in a file drawer somewhere. The idiographic acts of God may be in many scientists' file drawers.

Individual acts of God are idiographic, not nomothetic. Thus they belong in the humanities realm of knowledge (Chapter 2) and are outside the area science can investigate. Just as science cannot establish the truth of an individual historical event (although it can provide historical evidence), it cannot evaluate individual acts of God.

Personal Experience

Natural theology uses science, but personal experience has other knowledge-related possibilities. To consider personal experience as a source of knowledge, we must first distinguish it from scientific analyses involving personal experience. Now that cognitive psychology is a part of our paradigm, personal reports of cognitions can be used in psychology. These are scientific if they are replicated by others following the same procedures. Nevertheless, the result is still a result about human verbal behavior, not about the validity of the statements. A visual illusion is still a visual illusion despite the number of people that see the illusion. The fact that numerous people report astrology as giving accurate judgments does not make them accurate judgments. In fact, research shows that 90 percent are incorrect and they no more predict the future for the people with that sign than for people born under another sign (Kurtz & Fraknoi, 1996). Hence, the scientist must eliminate any claim to validity based solely on verbal report.

The labeling of these experiences as "personal" refers only to the experiences being from our own perspective. That perspective is shaped not only by what we see happening but also by the culture that gave us the assumptions by which we understand. Just as we saw in Chapter 2—Kuhn showing how much scientists are influenced by their subcultures—so we too can only interpret our personal experiences by the worldview provided by our subcultures.

The fact that our experiences are not automatically valid as science does not, however, mean that they are invalid as idiographic data and as spirituality. Consider my personal experience of climbing Mt. Shasta. That climb, for a nonathlete like me, was the toughest physical activity I ever did. I know from my experience that it was tough. However, this conclusion is not a scientific conclusion, for there is no way other investigators can follow the same method to elicit the same result from me. Even if they could induce me to climb that mountain again, it would be a different experience because of my earlier climb. Nevertheless, I still have knowledge of that climb.

The same distinction between personal experience and science occurs with many experiences related to spirituality. These are personal experiences, such as in the earlier exhibit about the movie *The Mission*. They are important sources of insight.

Actually, the history of science shows that science itself is based finally in each scientist's personal experience. As noted earlier, the original meaning of "experiment" centered on what we today call a "demonstration." When Pascal reported the results of taking a tube of mercury to the top of a mountain and finding the level less than at the foot of the mountain (because air pressure decreases with height), he was telling us how we could demonstrate this fact to ourselves. The failure of cold fusion was in the fact that other scientists could not replicate the effect in their own personal experience. This emphasis on personal experience in science has been long known. "One of the hallmarks of James' philosophy is its insistence on experience as the ultimate point of justification for any proposed truth" (Vanden Burgt, 1981, p. 56). James is clear as to "how reality is established. It comes to us in personal experiences based on direct experiences" (Gorsuch & Spilka, 1987, p. 775).

Of direct relevance to the spirituality necessary for integration to occur are several types of personal experiences that seem to push us beyond what science can discover. Among these are the categories of mystical experiences, near death experiences, and visits from a person who has recently died.

Mystical experiences are experiences that involve a feeling of unity with that which is greater than ourselves accompanied by a feeling of awe. It is distinctly different from how we usually feel. These experiences may range from the feelings we occasionally have with a beautiful sunset or on topping a hill and suddenly beholding a beautiful valley. Or they may be a deep experience in which a conversion takes that person to a new level of spirituality.

Most religious experiences of talking with or sharing with God are at least partially mystical. They have some of the basic elements but need not have all. For example, there may be the sense of the presence of another without a strong feeling of awe that accompanies the full mystical experience. It seems that the mystical experience is a continuum from the mystical experience to experiences of an almost everyday sort. For many the term "spirituality," which we are using in a broad sense, is closely identified with these experiences.

Mystical experiences have been only a limited part of the Judeo–Christian heritage of spirituality. Full mystical experience is not prominent in the Bible, although there are some major examples of it (e.g., Paul on the road to Damascus, Acts 9:1–19). Nor is it prominent in churches or in what most laity seek from worship. However, experiences such as a sense of God's presence in worship with feelings of love or awe are very common. Some would even say that spirituality does not exist without these type experiences. As with all mystical experiences, they are reported as central to one's religious faith and spirituality.

"Near death experiences" have been widely reported (Ring, 1980). They involve a feeling of leaving the body at the time when doctors consider them technically dead. Often these people report experiencing a tunnel of light and a decision as to whether to go back to their body. The number of the reports suggests that it is, in this sense, common. Such people, along with others with a close encounter with death, report a deepening spirituality (Ring, 1980).

Personal experiences of meeting a loved one after they have died have been reported. The deceased person in some form (not necessarily physical) pays them a short visit. This, too, occurs often enough to take seriously as reported experiences.

Both near death experience and meeting loved ones after their deaths are, however, absent from some traditional religions. Few experiences—some might say none—are reported in the Old Testament, and even the resurrection of Jesus is described differently than contemporary visits from departed loved ones. Hence these modes of knowledge, unlike other personal experiences, have restricted cross-cultural confirmation and may be the result of cultural assumptions of the people who have these experiences (for possible physiological explanations of near death experiences, see Blackmore, 1996).

Personal experiences can be very important, particularly of the mystical type. It is difficult to counter the person who says, "Sure God exists. I just talked with him this morning." Certainly, no general evidence will counter such experiences. Even if the skeptic argument is made—"How do you know that it was really God instead of your imagination?"—the answer is easily made: "The same way I know you exist. I really don't, but my personal experience leads me to have faith in the existence of both you and God." Personal experiences of this type allow spirituality to draw conclusions that are not testable by science.

What if psychologists could, through arranging the set and setting, produce a high rate of mystical experiences? Would that mean they are not spiritual experiences? No, it would just mean that psychologists have found ways to help people have spiritual experiences.

What if a specified set of neurological stimuli fed directly to the brain produced a mystical experience? Would that not "explain it away"? Only if one begins with a reductionistic assumption. Otherwise, it may be the source of spiritual growth for the person.

Let's consider the "worst case," one where it would be easy to argue that science "explains away" some aspect of spirituality because it finds conditions that lead to a particular spiritual experience. Let's assume that it is a case where we all agree the experience is illusionary. Does that make all such experiences illusionary?

To say that all experiences of X are illusionary because one set of conditions produces an illusionary experience of X is to generalize too broadly. An example is that of the Mulleur–Lyer illusion (see introductory psychology textbooks). It consists of a person judging which of two lines is longer. Under the conditions of the illusion, the wrong line is often selected as the longest. If finding a condition under which spirituality occurs that is illusionary means all spirituality were illusionary, then the Muller–Lyer illusion would show that all judgments of lengths of lines are illusionary. How could we ever agree with that? The conclusion is inappropriate because it is an overgeneralization. The proper conclusion is one that religious groups have long held: Spiritual criteria are established to distinguish between spirituality experiences to be taken seriously and illusionary spiritual experiences.

Note that the response of "you claim to have met God but I never have" is of little importance to establishing the existence of God. Few have met Paul and Betty Rathbun or Jess Moore either, and yet they were all important in my spiritual journey. Moreover, few would challenge their possible existence just because they have not had the pleasure of meeting them.

Why do people accept one individual's report of meeting person X (and therefore X's existence) and yet reject the same individual's report of the existence of God? The common response is that there is other evidence for the report of the other person. That other evidence involves either meeting person X ourselves or checking with others who have met person X. But the person who has experienced God is willing, indeed is generally eager, to help you meet God yourself. And that person can point to verbal and written reports from others who also claim to have met God. It does not seem that the level of evidence for the existence of others that I say I have met is much different from the same testimony for the existence of God.

The fact that some people have not met God has about as much bearing on the existence of God as the fact that I have probably not met you, the reader of this chapter, has on your existence. It is not relevant. A simple example may suffice to underscore this point. Mark and I were in the woods, and we had settled down to sit for a while. We watched several does come through the woods and pass a short distance from us, nibbling occasionally and walking slowly. Just after they topped the next rise, some people came noisily along the same path. It was apparent that they would never see the does since the does were keeping enough ahead of them to be out of sight. Later these people could correctly report that they had not seen any does, but it would be incorrect to then conclude that none were in the forest. In the same manner, not meeting God has no bearing on God's existence. Remember Templeton's (1997) statement: "Only arrogance would lead others to assert that what they cannot comprehend cannot exist" (p. 14).

Personal experience is a mode of knowledge different from the knowledge of science. Personal experience always has and always will be informed by our spirituality.

History

History is another mode of knowledge classically included in the humanities rather than the sciences. It is true that some parts can be scientific in that different investigators can examine the same material by the same method to see if replication occurs, but that is limited because the same historical events occur only once. No one doubts that history is about reality, but it is a mode of knowledge not included in science.

History builds on personal experiences and relies on human testimony. The former are just reports from one mode of knowledge, but history does add to it. History is the experience of a culture or cultures over time. It is known primarily by the multiple testimonies of people who have experienced it.

Sciences need to recognize that history can provide unique insights to the human condition, insights that have implications for spirituality. These insights help us put the possibilities of science into a broader perspective.

There is a similarity between science and history, and that is the desirability of multiple perspectives. A study of multiple histories of the same set of events provides a broader look at what may be truly valuable and workable. The fall of the Communist states shows that such a communal form is not a long-lived form of government. Many communal "utopias" were established in earlier years in the United States, but who can name one that has survived into current times? The fact that Christianity tried a communal form of living in the first century but gave no general recommendation for it is reinforcing of the conclusion from our century. Several such cases in different cultures and different times are mutually reinforcing. They help to provide understandings of worldviews that lay a more substantial base for integration. This is, of course, a base in addition to science.

Historical data, broadly defined, are a cross-validation of personal data. Given the breath of the historical data, we should be able to find parallels to any line of thought our personal experience suggests. If such are found, that allows us to perfect our thinking. Sometimes that perfection is to sharpen the issues, but it is often to find that there are problems as well. When history points to limits in our personal experiences, it helps us be humble.

Revelation

Revelation is the most unique mode of knowledge of the humanities. It is based on the assumption that we need help in finding the right and good, and that God has found a method of reaching us with that help. Whenever an aspect of spirituality is based on revelation the person believes is true, it has much more than personal experience and history to bring to the integration task with science.

The crucial question is whether such revelation has truly occurred. Just as in other areas, skepticism can doubt the validity of any revelation. The question for a decision is whether revelation is a reasonable explanation. This suggests that beliefs, attitudes, and values will all be important in that decision, but a clear argument for the truth of the revelation is needed. For that reason, in religious traditions the revelations long accepted across multiple cultures, such as those found in the Bible, are taken more seriously than one person's report of a personal revelation to just himself or herself.

What can revelation add to psychology? Basically, it can add answers for a spiritual base that transcends just our own culture and time and, if properly understood, can help us rise above ourselves. A crucial phrase is "if properly understood." Many serious debates arise around that issue and it is apparent that "proper understanding" is a very human process.

Our discussion of the evidence for the validity of revelation is of the Bible, in keeping with the declared commitment to Christianity from which this project has been undertaken. However, that evidence needs to be divided into two parts. On the one hand are the lines of reasoning that are considered by the person seeking to examine whether the Bible might be true. On the other hand are the internal evidences within the Bible; that is, its own statements as to its truth. The latter helps one to understand the message of the Bible, but only when at least a tentative commitment to the Bible being God's revelation is made.

As in so many areas in this book, the following is only a sketchy outline. Revelation is a detailed topic with many scholarly approaches.

The lines of reasoning that suggest the Bible be taken seriously even by those with little Christian background are several. My selection is somewhat arbitrary but, hopefully, also of contemporary relevance. First is scientific evidence, then historical evidence, and finally personal evidence.

The scientific evidence for the validity of the Bible lies in the meshing of its teachings with the human condition. Under the hypothesis that the God who created us is also the God who gave us the Bible, it should be a good guide to maximize human health and happiness. And so it seems to be. At the recent Conference on Spirituality and Health, scientists knowledgeable in their fields concluded that U.S. Christians have better physical health than U.S. non-Christians (there are too few of other religions to compare them against Christians) (Larson & Larson, 1994). This is accompanied by fewer mental problems and less substance abuse (Gorsuch, 1995). This is not to deny that there are occasional major failures in which a branch of Christianity is more harmful than helpful, for that certainly happens. Nevertheless, the major trends are clearly consistent with the hypothesis that the Bible contains principles that fit people well (assuming a culture with freedom of worship).

Of importance is what happens to human relationships when Biblical teachings are matched against what we are learning about people. Indeed, we could consider a very nonintuitive action urged by the Bible: loving and forgiving even enemies. This ideal is not widespread outside of Christianity. The concept of "Do unto others as you would have them do unto you" (Matthew 7:12) is a major step beyond the usual admonition to "not do unto others what you would not like them to do to you," for it is proactive rather than reactive. Further is the strange notion of "praying for your enemies" (Matthew 5:44) to be healthy and happy. Then we add to it "forgiving others 70 times 7" (Matthew 18:22), which clearly exceeds our capacity to even keep track of how often we have forgiven. While the research is just starting, it does appear that this behavior promotes strong and helpful human relationships (see, e.g., McCullough, Worthington, & Rachal, 1997; Enright & The Human Development Group, 1996; Meek & McMinn, 1997).

Psychology cannot answer the question of whether the Bible truly contains the word of God, for science's mode of knowledge is too limited (perhaps this is why people such as Freud or RBC must assume religion has no validity; they fail to see other modes of knowledge than just science). Therefore, we turn to history and personal experience as further ways of examining this claim.

The Bible is a historical document, claiming to report historical events. Outside evidence of the accuracy of that history is difficult to provide because few other sources have survived. Nevertheless, generally, the archeological evidence is strongly consistent with what the Bible reports.

It is true that studies of the Bible suggest that some books were written years after the events described, but that is not a serious problem for several reasons. Just note the number of books written hundreds of years after Columbus's journeys that are accepted as fact. The question is the source of the material and the expected accuracy of it, not when it was written.

For the Bible, studies do suggest that the sources included intermediate documents. For the first three Gospels, scholars believe that they shared a common source for many passages. Thus, while the Gospels were written years later, they were based in prior documents written closer to the events.

Then there is the fact of how oral traditions are kept alive. In societies that are mostly preliterate, more emphasis is placed on repeating the oral story exactly. The audience generally has heard the story so often that tellers of the story are corrected if they miss a word. Later those stories are written, and the document is virtually the same story as was told slightly after the event. That suggests that the Bible is accurate as to the history presented. Exhibit 3.2 gives a personal incident that set me to thinking about accuracy of the Biblical record and the passing years.

Exhibit 3.2
How Long Are Family Histories Accurate?

In Jerusalem I visited the place that was supposedly where Jesus was killed and buried. The tour guide noted that only tradition said that this was the actual place and no documents contemporary to the event existed that supported that place. The implication was that it was "just a tradition" and hence could hardly be taken seriously.

That set me to thinking. What we do know about the location is that Constantine built a church there almost 300 years after Jesus's death. That is a long time for an accurate memory to remain.

Some simple research turned up another interesting item. About A.D. 100 the Romans built a Roman temple on that spot to prevent the Christians from using it. Thus, the Christians in A.D. 90–100 identified it as the spot of Jesus's death and burial.

How accurate could the memories be of an event sixty years after it had taken place? Do any of your family memories trace back sixty years? We have some family memories that trace back to the civil war, 130 years ago. The events were trivial compared to Jesus's execution, but I have no reason to doubt their accuracy even though they are just based on family memories.

Some worshipers in A.D. 95 probably knew someone whose father, at least, was alive when Jesus died. That father could have taken his children and pointed out where it happened. Perhaps they were a part of those who worshipped there. Some of those children would be alive in A.D. 95, as well as grandchildren who had been shown the spot. Could the other worshipers have identified the wrong spot? If they had done so, the response would have been "No way! My (grand)father stood right here when it happened and the cross was right there!" The number of such testimonies would not need be many for the proper spot to be chosen.

Commentary: The odds that the wrong spot would have been chosen are long odds indeed.

Another clue to the Bible's historical accuracy is the range of materials it includes. Some, frankly, are embarrassing now and were even more so in the first century. On the cross, Jesus asks God, "Why have you forsaken me?" (Matthew 27:46). God forsaking his own son (or Jesus losing faith in God) is hardly the most socially desirable report that could have been written. Peter, who was a major leader in Jerusalem shortly before the New Testament writings, is often portrayed as a buffoon rather than as a "leader on the rise." We might take this as an effort by Peter's enemies to degrade him in favor of another leader, except that no other such leader is presented among Jesus's disciples. This is consistent with an emphasis on the accuracy of the reports.

Personal experience is also testimony to the validity of the Bible. There are many reports that reading the Bible has had a positive impact on people's lives. "Try it yourself—act as if you believe it is true" has long been a statement in support of the Bible. Some missionaries have told me that this approach is one of the most effective. Test it with your own experiences.

With an initial acceptance of the Bible, its contents become more important. How the contents are treated varies with the type of revelation the Christian believes best describes the Bible. These vary from the original copy of each book of the Bible being dictated by God, to the Bible containing the word of God that is the infallible guide for our lives, to the Bible being a human document recording the experiences of people interacting with God. But in any case, it provides benchmarks for spirituality that psychology is too limited to provide.

With the Bible as revelation, how do we look at psychology in particular and science in general? The results are descriptive. We must mix the proscriptive, the way God would like us to be, with the descriptive, the ways we have chosen to live. The Bible being God's revelation is the key to separating the mix, a task of which science is incapable. Revelation joins personal experience and history as a mode of knowledge unavailable to science. These modes are bases for spirituality's contributions to integration.

Might revelation be the basis of some particular psychological theory? Spilka and Bridges (1989) suggest there are parallels between theologies of the oppressed and social cognitive psychology. It may be that the value given to different aspects of the personality comes from spirituality. Of course, theology may suggest psychological hypotheses, but any psychological theory arising from spirituality is either a value statement beyond the limits of what science can investigate or is a theory to be tested as any other psychological theory.

Indeed, if honest revelation-based theology and honest science is done, we expect many areas of disagreement as well as agreement. When disagreement occurs, there are two points of which we must be aware. First, due to lack of human understanding both Biblical interpretation and science have many inconsistencies that may—if past history predicts future—never be reconciled. Both theologians and scientists are uncomfortable with the inconsistencies in their own disciplines and attempt to reduce them. Both find that many inconsistencies remain. Since both contain inconsistencies within their disciplines, why should we be surprised by inconsistencies between them?

The second point for disagreements between revelation and science is that of the model of integration. Christians relying heavily on the Bible as revelation may, when disagreements with psychology appear to arise, move from a model of "Christ and culture" to "Biblical interpretation over culture." The shift in the last sentence from "Christ" to "Biblical interpretation" is crucial. We never can be sure that we fully understand the meaning of revelation, and so if we override psychology because we feel it disagrees with revelation, we must always acknowledge that it is only our version of that revelation. A bit of humility is in order. Do I need to say that vice versa also applies? If we shift to a "culture over Christ" model, must we not also confess that it is our cultural understanding of that science that we are really using? And may not humility also be appropriate? Moving from an integrative model to a model in which either spirituality or science dictates to the other is done only at peril to the integrity of integration itself. Perhaps occasional inconsistencies are better than the alternatives.

DETERMINISM OR FREE WILL?

Determinism is the philosophical position that everything has its place in a causal chain of events. Each event is completely the product of prior events that cause that focal event. They may be difficult to completely understand due to multiple causes involved in any one event. Determinism holds for people as well as things. **Free will is the**

position that people are more than the products of prior events. Instead, people can shape their own lives if they wish. We shall take this question seriously, but there are other views of how we should treat these philosophical questions (Exhibit 3.3).

EXHIBIT 3.3
Beyondism on Unsolved Philosophical Problems

RBC (Cattell, 1987, p. 80) notes that the problem of free will versus determinism is one of several long-term philosophical problems. He states that both determinism and free will exist, although we cannot currently solve how they can do so.

Indeed, he warns scientists that one is tempted to go into philosophy when the data end. That is, however, "like a dog chasing a duck into a pond." It produces a lot of "verbal barking" that we may enjoy, but let us "not be deceived thereby into thinking we are getting substantially nearer to our quarry. Instead let us recognize that there are some questions that are best honestly and explicitly put on the shelf, until the human mind has *biologically* advanced beyond its present level" (Cattell, 1987, p. 81).

The lack of philosophical discussion is also a function of RBC's ethic. We have, in his eyes, many important data to collect, theories to develop and test, and applications to work out for the sake of our children and us. This is more important than debates that no one has solved despite centuries of trying.

Why May the Question Be Important?

The point of the free will versus determinism debate is that of, first, responsibility and, second, dominion. What happens to the field of ethics if all of our acts are determined? Surely we cannot blame anyone when the act done is determined by forces outside that person. And the idea of God giving us dominion is meaningless if all our acts are determined, for we could never exercise that dominion.

For a fruitful discussion, we must note what the free will position does not mean. It does not mean that choices are random; they will be based on the information the decider has. Free will decisions are always limited by our humanness. That includes that we cannot make decisions that are outside of the knowledge that we have. These points will become important later in discussing responsibility.

Note the logical paradox of determinism, for if everything is determined, then we are completely determined. The arguments for and against determinism are all equally determined. Then we can find no truth, for we only discover what we are predetermined to discover. So the person who argues for free will was predetermined to do so, and the person arguing for determinism was predetermined to do so regardless of its truth. But who wants to spend time analyzing a position that is predetermined regardless to its truth value? This takes us right back to Exhibit 3.3.

The question does pit two different paradigms against each other; these are based upon two different modes of knowledge. The scientific paradigm assumes there are regularities that can be understood. Classically science also holds that everything can be predicted once science is sufficiently advanced, and scientific data—replicable by independent observers—have demonstrated that much is indeed predictable from this model. Some then could draw the moral conclusion that we are not morally responsible. The notion that we are not responsible for what we do is illustrated in Exhibit 3.4.

Exhibit 3.4
Westside Story

In the 1961 musical *West Side Story*, several songs poke fun at some of our conceptions. These include one about delinquency. The boys tell the officer and the judge,
"Our mothers all are junkies."
"My parents treat me rough."
"My grandma pushes tea."
"I'm depraved on account of I'm deprived."
"It's not I'm antisocial, I'm just antiwork."
"We ain't bad, we're just misunderstood."
To which an observer replies,
"Sociologically he's sick!"
To which the social worker replies,
"This boy don't need a job, he needs a year in the pen!"
Commentary: When every condition is set against people, how can they be blamed for that which they do? But if they cannot be blamed, what happens to responsibility?

Spirituality, however, as noted earlier in this chapter, allows another mode of data in addition to science: personal experience. And the personal experience is that we have choices, make choices, and that these choices shape our lives. The humanities, including government, law, and ethics, presume responsibility can be given and that people can be held accountable.

The recognition that different modes of knowledge are involved does provide a possible resolution of the free will–determinism question.

We can note that science, to fulfill its purpose to "oversimplify reality so it can be comprehended by our minds," does not deal with all the modes of knowledge and so leaves out the evidence on free will. However, this is only a partial solution because we still would have the problem of how to match scientific determinism with the self-reports of free choice.

What Is Causation?

Crucial to the notion of determinism is the concept of causation. Determinism, in the sense that makes the debate with free will meaningful, involves causation.

An event is determined because it follows directly from its causes. In the experiment the experimenter adds salt to water and discovers that the salt causes the freezing point of the water to drop from 32 degrees F to 0 degrees F. This knowledge is applied in making icy and snowy roads safer: Salt is scattered on the road so the ice and snow will melt. We put the knowledge to use in exercising our dominion to reduce accidents.

While the example of spreading salt to melt ice is causation as we currently view it, causation itself has a wider and muddy history. It originates in the ancient Greek courts, and referred to judging a person responsible (Smith & Gorsuch, 1989). It developed into two meanings (1) the person responsible and (2) the intention behind it. A war was caused by (1) the series of incidents that led up to it and (2) the hopes or fears of those that went to war.

The notion of cause is not, then, necessarily a simple one. It can vary depending on the perspective taken. Is the perspective that of the incidents leading to the event or is it the hopes and fears that lead someone to choose that action?

Cause was seen by Aristotle (345 B.C./1990) in four different ways. Two of particular interest here are the efficient cause and the final cause. For a shoe, the efficient cause is the transformation of the materials into the shoe, the making of the shoe. The final cause is the end for which the shoe is made, and can probably best be determined by asking the one who buys it. Science deals in the former but spirituality deals in both.

Determinism is based on the science notion of causation, that of Aristotle's efficient cause. It follows from the experiment that considers only the efficient cause. Consider research on children's altruistic behavior. The child helps another child when the first child has been in the same situation and been helped. The experimenter provides this experience of being helped, which is the efficient cause. Or is it? Could not the causation be considered from a different time perspective? In this case, the child helps the other child because the parents gave permission and the random number table put the child in the experimental group rather than the control group. Or the cause is that the child was born one day too late to enter first grade in 1991 and so entered in 1992, or the family moved to this neighborhood because the interstate took out their old home, or Miss Gallagher's class was full and so the child was put in Mr. Goldstein's class. All these were necessary to produce that child's altruistic behavior and could be considered causes.

Could not the cause be considered to be the experimenter, since he or she provided the intervention? Could it be the grant that enabled the study? Or could it be the law that provided the grant monies? Need we go on?

Du Casse (1969) takes an interesting position on causation. He suggests that it comes from our personal experience of changing events around us. We pick up the salt shaker and put salt on our food. We caused the food to be salted. He suggests that all other notions of causation are generalizations from these personal experiences, and that we get into trouble when we generalize too far. Du Casse's approach applies to the experiment. The experimenter manipulates the independent variable and the dependent variable changes. Then the independent variable causes the dependent variable—or did the experimenter? Du Casse would say to be strictly correct we can only consider it as the experimenter.

It is for such reasons as the cause being defined by the perspective taken that some scientists refuse to talk of causation. What then happens to determinism? Since spirituality is concerned with causation in the moral sense, it is important to note the variations of causation in courts. Greek courts, as noted, distinguished between the human acts that caused an event and the motivations or intentions behind those acts. Modern jurisprudence also breaks cause into two types. The first, the human events that caused it, is virtually the same as the Greek, but the second cause differs. It is *sanctioning*, which refers to approval or responsibility in the sense of guaranteeing that an event would happen (Smith & Gorsuch, 1989). The distinction could be seen in the Nuremberg trials of war criminals after World War II. The soldier who shot the person as part of a firing squad caused, in the sense of being the efficient cause, the death of the prisoner. However, the sanctioning agent would be the officer that made the decision to execute the prisoner. The sanctioner was the one blamed in the war trials. Why? Because if the soldier had refused the assignment to the firing squad, another one would have carried out the sentence. This soldier was not necessary for the death to occur. However, the officer provided the essential order that guaranteed the death, and so was deemed guilty of the death. We have the odd situation that the soldier firing the bullet that killed the prisoner, the cause in the scientific sense, had no bearing on the death in a spiritual sense.

All the variety of definitions of cause noted here makes it difficult to either agree with or dispute determinism. For what are we disputing? What is determinism without a clear definition of cause? The confusion around the nature of causation means that the question of determinism itself is muddy. I am inclined to think that the question itself is poor. This opinion arises not only because of the problems in defining causation but is reinforced by the fact that the debate has continued so long with so little light shed on it. I suggest it is because causation itself is so difficult to define, and so the determinism question has no definition of the crucially important "cause" from which to work.

The problems of causation are acknowledged in recent science. Turner (1965) notes that "causality and causal laws are hardly mentioned in modern treatises of science" (p. 268). However, we must be clear that the basis of the problem is in the notion of causality, not in scientific results or theories. Some (e.g., Clayton, 1997) would make much of "indeterminacy principles" and "unpredictability" in physics as "proving" such issues or "allowing a place for God to act in the contemporary world," but these arguments must be taken skeptically. They have two problems. First, they take too seriously the determinism assumption, which has the problems already noted. Second, the history of science shows that what is unpredictable by the theories of one generation may be quite predictable from the theories of the next generation. To base any spirituality argument on the lack of current science to predict a phenomena is to base it on shifting sand, for tomorrow's bedrock may be found in the midst of that sand. Any such bedrock will leave unchanged the ambiguous nature of causality itself.

Interestingly, the concept of causation makes more sense for free will than for determination. Causation in the jurisprudence sense is essential for free will decisions to be judged. If we are responsible for our acts, then it makes sense to ask about intention as causation as in some Greek usage and about sanctioning as in some American usage. Without us being causes, spirituality has no way of assigning responsibility, by which ethical decisions are ethical.

The acts of God are better understood in the sense of cause as sanctioning or responsibility. God, in Christian theology, sanctions the health of an individual and wants that to happen, just as the person's family does. When that individual becomes sick, God sanctions the doctor who, possibly as a part of that doctor's spiritual commitment to healing, operates on that individual. If the doctor were not available, then perhaps God would have worked through another doctor or even spontaneous recovery. No matter how it happens, it could be God's answer to a prayer because God sanctioned it; that is, made sure it would happen. Christian spirituality assures us of that sanctioning; science may provide the details of how it was carried out in a particular case. Thus, the manner in which God achieves the recovery is just a detail.

The understanding of causation suggested here also helps to understand attributions to God. Craig Smith and I (Gorsuch & Smith, 1983; Smith & Gorsuch, 1989) found that people attributed causation to God in addition to causation to people. If we asked the degree to which person A was the cause of a life being saved and the degree to which God was the cause, a respondent often considered A to be 50 percent and God 75 percent at the same time. The total causation was over 100 percent. That is quite reasonable in light of the prior paragraph's conclusions about the nature of causation being one of scantioning and responsibility.

Newton, it appears, had no trouble at all with God as the causative power behind natural events. As Davis (1996) has pointed out, the "Newtonian mechanistic" universe was not Newton's universe. He saw each natural law as an expression of God's activity in this world. God acts in the world at all times, as in matter attracting at a distance. The world is the result of God's divine action, and so experimentation is a method of seeing what God is doing. The fact that an event could be considered 100 percent caused by prior events and 100 percent attributable to God would have been natural to Newton.

The approach suggested here—that God is a cause even of events 100 percent predictable—is consistent with our definitions of responsibility and the problems of defining causation in science. It does, however, call into question one approach to natural theology. That approach, called the "god of the gaps" approach, is to take a completely deterministic view that reserves causation for science. So if science finds a cause, then God could not be a cause. God is only seen in action if the event cannot otherwise be explained by science. Thus, a gap in science is filled with God. As science expands, God's sphere of action must contract. As "universal principles of the unseen world that can be determined and tested by extensive examination of human behavior and other data" (Templeton, 1995, p. 118) are found, then theology looses that ground as well. A "god of the gaps" theology, however, forces theologians to claim only areas science cannot currently predict as the source of God's action. As those areas are reduced, then God's action can no longer be claimed for them. Theology looses to science (including to psychology).

The most recent such rationale is to take the current unpredictability of quantum physics as the place of God's action (Murphy, 1995). For example, God would answer prayer to cure a cancer by juggling the unpredictable quantum events is such a way that they would "snowball" up the chain of events until the cancer disappears. Peacocke (1993) realizes that "god of the gaps" theologies are vulnerable to the advance of the natural sciences, and so proposes that God be found in the "permanent gaps in our ability to predict events in the natural world. . . . There would be no fear of such a God being squeezed out by increases in scientific knowledge" (p. 153). Peacocke then raises serious theological objections to this position.

Basing God's action in the "permanent gaps" of prediction is based in a feeble hope that an unpredictable area of science will always be unpredictable. Chaos theory, for example, takes chaotic areas that were unpredictable and shows how they can be predicted in theory. And the fact that quantum theory cannot predict if Schrodinger's cat will be found to be dead or alive when the box is opened only means that it cannot be predicted by the current theories of science. Murphy (1995) hedges her bets by suggesting it is what is now (quantum events) or in the future (something yet unknown) at the bottom of causation (but that still seems to have the problems of a "god of the gaps" rationale). She also suggests that God acts through people by influencing the "stimulation of neurons" (p. 394). However, this can, again, only be held until science has laws explaining such firing, and so is another "god of the gaps" theology.

Basing God's action in the "permanent gaps" of prediction as identified by physics—such as quantum physics, Heisenberg's uncertainty theorem, or firing of neurons—is based on the assumption that current science is able to identify what scientists can never do. That is a dubious assumption. By some 1920s theories of physics, scientists predicted that the atom would never be split, and we know how wrong that prediction was. Templeton (1995) notes that while three predictions of relativity theory were substantiated, many others were not. Science knows what it has substantiated; science does not know what the next generation will discover. Hence, basing God's action in uncertainty principles and quantum physics is just another "god of the gaps" theology, and a very weak approach to natural theology; it will sooner or later again lose to science.

However, one is only forced into a "god of the gaps" theology if determinism is assumed to be at the heart of science. Since in the present postmodern approach classical determinism is not a viable concept, there is no need of a "god of the gaps" approach. This is, of course, compatible with most current theologies, which see God as immanent, creating, and involved; at the same time theologies view science (including psychology) as exploring what God is about.

Does Our Answer to the Free Will Question Make a Difference?

In addition to our personal experience that makes the free will option seem sensible and in addition to the needs of our legal system, there are psychological theories that say that our answer to this question makes a difference. There are several lines of research that point to our belief in our free will being a critical factor in our living in accordance with our spirituality. Here are some of them:

- The correlation between people's values and their behavior changes depending on their acceptance of responsibility for their acts. Those who feel they have no such responsibility have little correlation between their values and their behaviors. Those who feel they are responsible have a much higher correlation between their values and their behaviors (Aleshire in Gorsuch, 1984).
- There are different ways of coping with adversity. The type that relates most to better outcomes is that in which the person engages in coping. Better yet is coping in which they engage the problem working with God and in active service to God's will (Pargament, 1997; Wong-McDonald & Gorsuch, 1997).
- Learned helplessness is a condition in which the person learns that they can do nothing to affect their outcomes. That does not bode well for the future (Meyers, 1999).

From a spiritual perspective, when we assume causation, free will, and responsibility the outcomes are consistent with those assumptions. We make free will decisions for which we are held responsible.

Conclusions

At this point we can suggest several conclusions:

1. The concept of determinism is in doubt because the concept of cause is in doubt when applied to science.
2. Causation is best defined as our feeling of control when we make a decision and act; science helps us have that control.
3. Causation in the sense of conclusion 2 is necessary for free will to be meaningful and for us to act on our values.
4. Causation in the sense of responsibility is necessary for spirituality to give meaning to praise and punishment.
5. Causation appears to make most sense in understanding our dominion over the world and ourselves; that is, as a part of spirituality.

Integration of spirituality with psychology does not appear to be hampered by the determinism versus free will debate when understood as shown here. May I again suggest that any question debated for thousands of years but whose possible answers seem unrelated to any behavior should be low on our priorities?

EVIL

While we might think that the nature and existence of evil is a basic given, science has proceeded without assuming that evil exists. This is workable because science is basically descriptive. Christianity (as well as other worldviews) sees evil as a real and necessary category.

As noted in discussing determinism, psychology as classical science has little place for ethical choice. Hence, it has little place for assignments of right or wrong, and thus for identifying evil. The most hideous crime is a result of natural developments just as much as the life of a saint.

The continuing debate about whether scientists should carry out particular lines of research and whether they should be blamed for how the information from that research is used are questions about integration, not about science. Science has no way of answering these questions. Nevertheless, as noted early in this book, scientists are people with their own worldviews and those worldviews do influence their research. Scientists chose what research to pursue, and that choice comes from their spirituality or lack thereof. In that sense, scientists are responsible for the lines of research they pursue and for any predictable impact of their results.

No one can foresee all the uses of any development, and so scientists cannot be criticized if the science is used in a wrong or evil manner different than immediately projected. Nor can a scientist be criticized for a serendipitous result that then becomes misused. Serendipitous results are, by definition, not predicted at the time the experiment is carried out.

The scientist is, however, responsible for whether the results are published. As a graduate student I accidentally saw correspondence between RBC and another leading personality researcher, both of whom had independently found a relationship between an easily observed physical characteristic and another variable. The correspondence was about their both deciding that publishing that fact would produce prejudicial treatment of some people. Publishing the finding would, in their judgment, produce more harm than good so they agreed to just forget the results.

While it is good to say that the scientist should just not publish results that could be misused, it is generally not that easy. On the one hand, the proper use may have many benefits. On the other hand, it is likely that someone else will find the same result soon. Since science is built by a body of scientists, results found by one person will probably be found by someone else also participating in that research program. One person not publishing the result has no long-term effect except to eliminate the scientist who did not publish it from the debates about the uses of the results. If the nonpublisher is the more integrated scientist, is reducing the likelihood of that person's being in the debate ethical?

There are some ways that science gives information that is taken as defining the good. For example, the disruption of normal development can be easily seen, from the viewpoint of almost all worldviews, to be a problem. All children should have enough nutrition to not affect physical stature or mental development. Major disruptions of mental functioning, such as psychoses, are to be corrected. Note, however, that even these cases have a supporting worldview that gives the value judgments.

Beyond simple cases, psychology provides no help, but its implicit view is that of a neutral universe. No assumption of the universe being "for us" or "against us" is needed or allowed. Indeed, since the universe is inanimate it can neither "care" nor "make decisions." Everything happens by inanimate objects interacting with each other. No such thing could possibly have any "personal attitude" or "make a decision" about us. This differs from the position taken by most spiritualities.

When does science's neutrality become a problem? When it is extended to become a worldview itself without consideration of science's limitations in this regard. What most people judge as evil is not really judged at all by science. Instead, the evil is, to science, just another phenomena to be examined and described. That encourages a neutral fatalism that is opposed by most spirituality. Spirituality involves a choice for that which is good.

The worldviews of some tribes is that the world is full of dangers, often personified in "evil spirits." The movie *The Mission* portrays one such tribe. When they had the choice of abandoning their new village life with the missionaries or fighting a battle they would probably lose, they choose the latter. To return to the jungle and the constant presence of evil spirits was not worth it.

The Judeo–Christian worldview has a place for both good and evil, with an optimistic faith in the outcome. The "powers and principalities" and "demons" of the New Testament are ignored by most U.S. theologies but have a major place in Third World theologies. Most people in the world feel that they have seen or felt evil as an active, powerful force. One of the differences between U.S. and Third World theologies of evil probably arise from our more extensive use of science to describe and explain bad events, as noted in Exhibit 3.5.

EXHIBIT 3.5
Is My Germ Your Evil Spirit?

The story is told of a missionary from the United States working with a Third World tribe. Teaching the theology was going well. The missionary, being concerned with the whole person rather than just the soul, also taught good health practices, such as boiling water before drinking it. When asked the purpose of boiling water, the missionary explained about germs. The reply was "But I thought you told us there were no evil spirits."

Commentary: What is the difference between a germ and an evil spirit? It appears that the only real difference is that a germ cannot be changed by talking to it. For germs and evil spirits are alike in being invisible to the unaided human eye and in advancing themselves at our expense!

Science's problem with good and evil is that science is descriptive rather than prescriptive, as already noted. Descriptions only tell what is and what might be, not what should be. In order to use the results of science, integration with some type of spirituality—at least ethics—is necessary. That integration usually happens by laws that encourage or discourage particular uses of science. The regulations for nuclear power plants is another example. Still another is that genetic changes in crops must meet certain standards to prevent a genetic disaster from occurring. These standards are established by society's laws, and so are an integration of science and society's worldview. As yet little investigated is the question of what laws are needed to encourage and discourage poor uses of psychology.

Pollution and the developing disasters from overpopulation are signs that unfettered use of science creates problems unless thoughtfully evaluated. Every culture requires the larger view of what the world should be that ethics, philosophy, theology, and other aspects of spirituality can provide. Of course, different spiritualities may stress different decisions at any point. Those spiritualities stressing the equality of people with the rest of nature may have different recommendations than those giving humans some dominion.

Bringing in a society's worldview means that ethical judgments using information from science are open to the same ethnocentric biases that plague all judgments by human groups. Such biases are independent of the quality of the science, but can lead some to think that science itself has made a spiritual point. The biases can only be examined and debated when it is realized that the ethical judgments using the science are judged by spirituality standards, not scientific standards. A corollary is that scientists debating the ethical use of their discoveries are not necessarily the best people to judge the use of that science; the best people to do so are those who understand the possible spiritual implications of that science.

In response to ethnocentric bias that can warp the integration of science and spirituality is a Christian response: Use the Bible to guide the integration. For both nonbelievers and believers, the Bible has the advantage of coming from a radically different culture. The land base was small, the people were few, the predominant economic system was nonmercantile herding and farming, and the people were isolated. This is radically different from the present, from the size of English-speaking countries, from the hundreds of millions in the country and the millions in a city, from the money-based industrial economy, and from our "global village." Hence, the Bible is an excellent check on our cultural biases. It also has the advantage of being extensively studied so that we can put its events into context.

For the believer the Bible has a stronger advantage: It is the basis of his or her spirituality since it reveals the principles God would have him or her follow. What better base for spirituality and integration with psychology could one have than that?

EXERCISE

Here are some possible causes of a science–spirituality conflict:

- Different sources of knowledge.
- Spirituality assuming its knowledge base extends into science.
- Science assuming its knowledge base extends into spirituality.
- Use of different sciences.
- Use of different spiritualities.

Where have you noticed a conflict between science and spirituality? What was a major source of that conflict?

CHAPTER 4

Psychology: Suggestions for Worldviews

Chapter 3 pointed to limitations of sciences such as psychology from the perspective of spirituality. But Integration Commentary goes both ways. What can psychology say about limitations in worldviews, spirituality, and theology, given the integration proposed by this project?

Since psychology is rather new to discussions of this type, the first section of this chapter outlines the need for a two-way dialogue. The next section introduces specific issues that arise from human thought processes and reasonable decision making, some of which limit the theology of spirituality. How, then, can scholars interested in spirituality use psychology in general for its contribution to integration? Are there methods by which those interested in spirituality can engage psychologists for an integrative solution to spiritual problems?

BASES FOR TWO-WAY DIALOGUE

For a two-way dialogue to occur it is important for those whose primary concern is spirituality to have a preliminary knowledge of psychology. Certainly, the psychologist needs some exposure to spirituality as well, but it appears that psychologists with such interests have been more involved in religious thinking and practices than theologians have been with psychology. Of course, this will vary widely from one scholar to another, but the point is that there needs to be some common understanding of the social science with which integration is to occur.

A limitation in dialoguing with psychology is the technical nature of psychological literature. Unfortunately, some spirituality scholars have turned to only that psychology which a psychologically uneducated person can read in the original, such as Freud and Jung. These are important historical figures, but over three-quarters of a century has past since they wrote. To say that they are out of date is an understatement. The vast majority of psychology's history occurred after those writers. Naturally their writings are of occasional interest outside of historical analysis, but a quick glance at psychological journals and textbooks indicates that is rare. They are almost never referenced except as historical figures. Instead we turn to contemporary writers who represent the movements that developed out of the earlier contributions.

Instead of reading out-of-date literature, the scholar needs a basic understanding of contemporary psychology. I hope that they can obtain that by at least taking a minor in psychology or doing the equivalent independent study. Part of that background needs to be an introduction to psychological methods and statistics if the scholar wishes to read original documents. Or it may be that two degrees are necessary if one wishes to not just read integration literature but help build it; this is the model for my training and that of my students. Their doctorates are in psychology, but they have at least a master's in theology also.

The primary psychological research articles will seldom be accessible to the scholar in spirituality. Not only are they very technical, they only report one study. That study can only be interpreted when the context of that part of the discipline is known. For integration, we need to find and use well-replicated phenomena of psychology. A literature search of articles does not answer that need. However, there are other materials that do give general findings in psychology that would be of interest to a broader group. Exhibit 4.1 summarizes several such sources.

EXHIBIT 4.1
Sources of Psychological Knowledge
for the Nonpsychologist

There are several sources of well-replicated psychological materials that may be of interest to scholars from other disciplines. The resources provide broader views, of varying technical sophistication, than individual articles.

Books. Books are able to develop a line of reasoning in greater detail than articles and can summarize many research studies instead of just one. They are the best introduction to the psychological paradigm in an area of interest. General texts such as introductions to social psychology or another area of interest are essential knowledge. Introductions to the psychology of religion (Paluzian, 1996; Spilka, Hood, Hunsberger, & Gorsuch, in press; Pargament, 1997) on coping summarize considerable useful psychology for integration. Check to be sure that any book is actually psychology, not pop culture, by checking the references. Look for books referencing psychological journals.

Journals for more general audiences. The *American Psychologist* and the *Psychological Observer* are the flagship journals of the American Psychological Association and the American Psychological Society, respectively. Both contain articles written for the broad audience of psychology, and hence are not technically oriented. They provide the information that one area of psychology wishes to communicate, not just within that area but to psychologists of other specialties and general readers. The *Journal for Social Issues, Contemporary Psychology*, and *Psychological Bulletin* are also of this type. Examing a couple of years of these five journals will give an excellent overview of current developments; examining earlier issues will provide a sense of the more permanent contributions.

The following two sets of materials assume the reader knows the general paradigm of that particular area. That is learned from the two previous types of resources.

Meta analyses. Once the mentioned materials have provided the paradigm and vocabulary of an area, meta analyses are a major source of knowledge. Well-replicated facts and principles in psychology are now primarily identified by this special technique. No individual study can produce a fact, since a fact must be replicated and so can only be established by several studies. Meta analysis identifies results that have been replicated. It statistically summarizes numerous studies on one issue and tests whether variations in the results occur, for example, only because the number of people in the studies varies. While the center sections of such articles are dense, the introductory and concluding sections usually provide an excellent summary and overview of what is established. These articles are essential for dialoging with psychology.

Annual Review of Psychology. To obtain an overview of recent work in an area, the *Annual Review* is helpful. Each article is by an acknowledged expert. Be aware that it is written for scholars in that area, but it does provide a good overview of what is happening (although not necessarily the results). It also identifies key articles if you wish to examine the original sources.

Commentary: Note that a popular fad is always to be skeptical about other psychologists' findings with a concern for only the current discussions. The most recent work is covered well in textbooks, but some work of a couple of decades earlier is dropped. It is dropped not because of contrary findings but because no one is actively researching it. However, that work may be of great importance in a particular setting. The level of current activity in an area is a poor measure of its possible relevance for spirituality. In fact, a serious worker may wish to examine older undergraduate texts in specialized areas to identify solid material that is not currently being investigated.

For a finding to be sufficiently solid to be a basis of integration, it must be well replicated. If it is the conclusion of a meta analysis, then it is well replicated. If it has not been tested over time, it may be "shifting sand." Watch for studies with a meta analysis; otherwise look for studies clearly replicating the findings over a decade or more. (Note that the number of references in an area only indicates the popularity of the area, not whether it has found anything.)

A temptation is for a scholar to begin doing the other discipline rather than dialoging with it. "Doing it" is when the spirituality scholar becomes, in effect, a psychologist. The materials of psychology are appropriated and repeated, with perhaps a slight change in terms to make them sound more spiritual. This, however, is appropriation rather than integration.

What we psychologists need from spirituality is guidance on spiritual issues. For example, what is the nature of the good for situation X? We need this in part because we psychologists are tempted to jump from knowing, for example, characteristics of people at age thirty to stating that people with such characteristics are "more mature." This is particularly problematic because it can be done without noticing that we have shifted from a psychological observation to a normative statement. Unfortunately, spirituality scholars may then accept the psychologist's conclusion as if they were fact based rather than worldview based. More involvement of philosophers and theologians is needed along with psychologists. It helps keep us honest.

Special Note

Since this project is an introduction to integration with only examples of how it is done, the psychology is quite selected. The examples of psychological knowledge were selected to have relevance for integration, of course. But in addition they were selected as well-replicated basic principles that have wide impact, although their presence in undergraduate books in exactly the form stated here was not a selection criterion. In addition, the selections were required to be easily communicated.

THOUGHT PROCESSES AND REASONABLE DECISION MAKING FOR SPIRITUALITY

On the Limits of Decision Making

A major limitation on spirituality scholars is the limits of human judgment. These apply to all of us. But a temptation of spirituality is to absolutize our own human judgments.

I have often appreciated the distinction scholars make between scriptures such as the Bible and theology as sources of God's wisdom. These theologians conclude that the Bible contains the Word of God, but they do not reach the same conclusion about theology itself. The implication is that theology is a human discipline, so we need be careful to avoid confusing it with "ultimate truth."

The limits of human judgment also apply to studies of spiritual documents, but with a special consideration. Unlike science, where we can gather new data to test theories, a spiritual document such as the Bible is a given and there is no way to obtain new verses. This means that historical and theological analyses proceed, but without the safeguard science has from replication.

Scriptures such as the Bible also have another problem for scholars. It is a document we know well before we begin formal study of it. And certainly scholars in the middle of a career know it very well. That means that all hypotheses are after the fact; that is, ex post facto. Unfortunately, as seen in Exhibit 4.2, it is easy to develop interpretations ex post facto. Biblical analysis is therefore inherently limited by its ex post facto nature.

Exhibit 4.2
Making Sense of Nonsense

I was computing some analyses in a multischolar research study. The results were not as expected. When I showed them to my colleague, he stopped and thought for a while. Then my colleague suddenly said, "I know what it is!" He proceeded to give a reasonable rationale to explain the finding.

I also had a hypothesis about that result. I checked the data entry and found that a number had been entered as 32 instead of a 23. I corrected the datum and reran the analysis. The original result disappeared but another finding appeared.

The results were not as expected. When I showed them to my colleague, he stopped and thought for awhile. Then my colleague suddenly said, "I know what it is!" He proceeded to give a reasonable rationale to explain the finding.

Several studies have given labels randomly to data developed for another purpose. The "results" were then shown to experts in the area. They consistently come up with good explanations *even for random data*. I have occasionally tried this with a class, and we could quickly find a way to fit even unusual data into a reasonable explanation. This is such a prevalent tendency that one of my definitions of an expert is "a person who can make any result in the area of that person's professional expertise fit a theory."

I have considered using this procedure on final oral exams for a doctorate. We would give random labels from the student's area to data and ask the student to interpret them. If they could not come up with an interpretation even for ridiculous random data, then I would know that they were not of the same caliber as those already in the area. (I have never done this because it seems that some are so impressed with their interpretation they considered it fact!)

Commentary: Are Biblical scholars any less experts in their areas than psychologists are in theirs? If not, then they are also capable of finding excellent ex post facto interpretations.

Science sets hypotheses before seeing the data and requires replication to prevent our developing conclusions when there is really nothing there. Biblical analysis is open to the same problems as analyses of other data. However, there is no method for testing the conclusions reached because of the lack of new data.

Research methods are designed to reduce the alternative explanations that could be given for a result (Campbell & Stanley, 1963). The results are also examined by journal reviewers for the possibility of an alternative explanation that has been overlooked in the study. That is acknowledged in the article's discussion section (or when pointed out by another scholar), and another study is developed to remove even that alternative explanation. This is not, of course, new. Thomas Aquinas would set out his proposition and then follow that with the possible challenges to it. Only when all the other possibilities had been removed from contention was Aquinas ready to entertain the possibility of the theory being supported.

Exhibit 4.3 illustrates possible explanations for some widely discussed variations in the Bible. Read the first two paragraphs and stop. Can you think of another possible interpretation? The rest of the exhibit lists the alternative explanations that have occurred to me over the years.

Exhibit 4.3
Alternative Explanations: New Testament Examples

In analysis of the New Testament, the question has been raised as to whether the same writer, such as Paul, wrote several passages attributed to him. Is a particular letter, such as First Corinthians, actually one letter or has it been pieced together from several letters (possibly by several authors)?

The method is to compare sections for usage of the same or different words or for the usage of particular sentence structures. The comparison is useful because a given individual tends to write the same way time after time. Therefore, if another document said to be by that person uses a different vocabulary or sentence structure, the authorship is challenged.

Can you develop some alternative explanations for why words used or style might vary even with the same writer?

There are several alternative explanations for differences in vocabulary or writing style that need to be eliminated before accepting the conclusion of different authors in the New Testament:

1. The makeup of one congregation to whom Paul was writing may have differed from another, at least in how they talked about the faith. Paul wrote in the language of the recipients. Hopefully we all write differently to, for example, a grade school audience than how we write to our friends.

2. The letters were transcribed by different scribes. Scribes were the highly educated people of their time. As a good executive secretary does now, they may have improved Paul's writing as they went along. The differences in vocabulary and sentence structure are from the different scribes used.

3. As Paul was writing to, for example, the Corinthians, he had several other Christians present. They made suggestions that Paul incorporated. So different words and phrases were used depending on who made the suggestion that Paul used.

These three alternative explanations describe the same observed data, differences in letters as to vocabulary and sentence structure. They are just as reasonable as the notion of multiple authors, unless data or rationale are produced to the contrary. Since the single-author interpretation is more elegant than a multiple-author interpretation, it is to be preferred unless there is clear positive evidence to the contrary.

Of course, the authorship questions make little difference to those who hold the Bible to be inspired. God, who knew Paul better than we, may have wanted a scribe to do some rewriting. Certainly, God would welcome that for some contemporary writers. Perhaps that is part of how God was able to use fallible people for revelation.

Frankly, I find it difficult to keep a straight face when scholars seriously debate "which are the words Jesus really said" (Funk, 1998) or "this part of the verse is from Paul but not the last part of it." The task of making such decisions has not yet, to my knowledge, been proven possible, at least with the procedures commonly used. First, the explanations are ex post facto. Second, there are too many alternative explanations that could explain the data. Unfortunately these scholars have not realized some limits of human judgment that psychologists have been forced to acknowledge. Without that realization, it is easy for us humans to assume we know more than we really know.

Exhibit 4.3 does not mean that all historical studies of the Bible are doomed to failure. To separate out the more trustworthy from the less trustworthy we fall back on the notion of replication by others, even though they hold different worldviews. There are many points of scholarship that come to the same conclusion about the Bible, at least to the data. For example, the theory of different strands in the Old Testament from a "northern Israel" and "southern Israel" perspective is based on data to which almost all agree (even if they object to the "northern–southern" interpretation). Some passages talk of events happening in the North while other passages talk of events happening in the South, and these two traditions use different names for God. These and several other associated characteristics are readily seen (Welhausen, 1957). The point is that there are limits to what can be done with a preset database, such as the Bible, but valid work can be done within those limits.

It is in situations such as this that the question of the degree of objectivity needs to be carefully considered. High rater agreement does mean that some objectivity has been achieved in most scientific research. But it is a problematic criterion when applied to preexisting data, such as the Bible, for which people already have a position. The conviction that our judgments made before we examined the data may well determine our answers. Then objectivity would be from within a particular paradigm. But the only difference between this and objectivity in psychology is the existence of multiple contradictory paradigms. Spirituality should bring to the dialogue of integration only what can be reasonably done.

The Dangers of Ethnocentrism

Ethnocentrism is universally found in all groups. It is a major contributor to conflict (Chapter 6). Ethnocentrism is also a major problem for decisions being reached within any group, including the most spiritual. The more unique and spiritual a group feels themselves to be, the more likely ethnocentrism is to occur.

Ethnocentrism boils down to the conviction "we are better than they." It is a much stronger effect than one would expect and operates at even the slightest identifying of group membership. For example, people evaluate photographs of people for whom they know only that they are "in group A" or "in group B." The ones that are in the group to which the rater is randomly assigned are rated as better. The more salient the group membership, the more likely people are to judge their group better than other groups (R. Brown, 1995; Tajfel, 1981). This means that spirituality groups—whether or not they are formal religions—are inclined to hold their judgments of themselves higher than they should.

Certainly, we have all seen or read how spirituality groups can convince themselves that they and only they are correct. At the extreme, such convictions have been the bases of inquisitions within such groups and oppression and terrorism toward those outside those groups. In Christianity spirituality groups form the basis of denominations, each of which was founded to be a better form of Christianity, although they all feel they are the best. Some of these groups have held mutually contradictory positions—such as infants should be baptized or only adults can be baptized—and it is apparent that all could not be correct. Many of these have brought harshness into the lives of others, a harshness that seems more akin to evil than to spirituality.

How dangerous can ethnocentrism be? Baumeister (1997) has analyzed evil from a psychological perspective, summarizing numerous research studies. He concludes that there are several types or sources of evil, including material greed, threatened egotism, and the rare but still too frequent sadistic pleasure. Baumeister adds another source of evil based in ethnocentrism: idealism. "When people believe firmly that they are on the side of the good and are working to make the world a better place, they often feel justified in using strong measures against the seemingly evil forces that oppose them. Noble ends are often seen as justifying violent means. In reality, such means often discredit and contaminate the noble goals, but this outcome is rarely anticipated" (p. 377). Unfortunately, events in the news do and will continue to illustrate this point all too well.

While we can agree that ethnocentrism is a danger, are we not usually convinced that we and our group would seldom make such a mistake, and if we did that it would only be a small mistake? I am reminded of the Milgram experiments (Milgram, 1974; see Meyers, 1999, for a good overview). In these experiments people were found to be unexpectedly cruel to another if an authority figure asked them to do so. Milgram's most frightening conclusion is that all of us could be convinced, when we respect our group's leaders, to be agents of pain.

Ethnocentrism exists as a part of each and every group. While it is easy to recognize it among Christians, that is only because there has been a large number of Christians across a long history. Any other spiritual tradition that exists across such time periods and has such large numbers will also have groups that conclude they are the best group in that tradition while holding positions radically different than other groups within that tradition. Only by recognizing ethnocentrism's constant presence can we maintain our groups and yet hope to offset this bias.

Correcting for ethnocentric bias is a difficult task. Some try to do so by objecting to the group or subculture in which they were raised. If their subculture was for a strong military, then these people are for pacifism. If their subculture was for using scientific technology in farming, then they are for using only food grown with natural fertilizers. The only problem is that such people form their own subgroups, and like all groups they have ethnocentric bias, overvaluing themselves and their positions.

Perhaps Christian denominations serve a useful purpose in helping us recognize our ethnocentric bias. With so many different interpretations, including variations upon variations upon variations, it is hard to hold that any group has access to the "real truth." Perhaps this is why so many Christians hold the Bible to contain the infallible Word of God but never state that any theology reaches that level. We each, of course, believe our particular theology and denomination are correct; if we didn't, we would change it. Nevertheless, denominations can be a constant reminder to us that other thoughtful, spiritual people will disagree with us, and *they could be right*. Humility is a Christian virtue that every spiritual group needs.

American denominations seem to have covered all the major possible Biblical interpretations that are congenial with the current Western worldview. There is even a denomination for those who argue strongly we should be less denominational and more humble (Exhibit 4.4).

Exhibit 4.4
The Christian Church (Disciples of Christ)

"How presumptuous for one denomination to see itself as THE Christian church. If American denominations teach us anything, their existence should teach us that none can claim exclusive rights to being THE Church. There are just too many thoughtful people who disagree on this or that."

This is a common reaction to the denominational name in the title of this box. However, the comment comes from ignorance rather than knowledge of this rather unique group. This denomination was the one in which I was raised and with which—given my college studies of "cogito ergo sum," philosophy, and psychology—I choose to continue.

The Disciples of Christ began in the early 1800s as a uniting movement rather than a separatist movement. The leaders held, and continue to hold, that the multiple divisions seen in American denominations are "hair splitting," even when our sight is often too poor even to recognize the hair, let alone split it. What we need to do first is recognize that such infighting does no good, either for our spirituality or for our ideas. Second, we need to practice "in essentials, unity; in non-essentials, liberty; in all things, charity (love)" (Campbell, 1835/1975).

What are the essentials of Christianity? Those that all Christian denominations recognize as valid, and that anyone reading the Bible can clearly find there. These include God's forgiveness for each of us, a rejection of legalism, the centrality of Christ, the centrality of the Bible, and loving and forgiving others. Note that this identifying essentials that almost all Christian groups agree on is a theological version of replication; if the different denominations all see X as Christian, then X is appropriate within this denomination. (Of course, given ethnocentricity effects, we have as hard a time living this principle as do others with their creeds.)

As Disciples, we hold that "All those who follow Christ are Christians." So we hold that there are the Christian Church (Roman Catholic), the Christian Church (Presbyterian), the Christian Church (Church of God), and so on.

And there is the Christian Church (Disciples of Christ).

Commentary: Since I was raised in the Disciples of Christ, I must give them the credit for my feelings that theologians need an emphasis on replication, just as do scientists. I am happy to acknowledge that debt, but suspect I have occasionally downgraded the quality by letting some of my own ideas intrude. Ideas come from the paradigms that our cultures give us, and we just hope we can enhance them somewhat so that others may also benefit from the best of our paradigm, and learn from the worst.

All concerned with spirituality need to approach their tasks with humility. With the limits of human judgment and the distortions of ethnocentrism found by psychology, we must be cautious about the conclusions we draw. It is, of course, still necessary that we make decisions for ourselves on issues for which we know our judgments are fallible. Nevertheless, when our decisions impact other's lives we must recognize that, despite our best intentions, our decisions could be wrong. It is all right to bet our own lives on our conclusions, but we should be very careful about betting other's lives.

DIALOGING WITH PSYCHOLOGY TO
ACHIEVE SPIRITUAL GOALS

In Chapters 3 and 4 Commentary Integration has been the task. In Chapter 1 Joint Problem Solving also was noted as a type of integration. What can spirituality expect from psychologists that might be a helpful basis for joint problem solving?

A Warning

In integrating with psychology we need to recognize biases that exist in much of psychology, particularly the reduction of spirituality to personal needs. Psychology generally ignores beliefs and treats spirituality as only motivation. Freud was a prime example of such bias, and R. B. Cattell has shown the same propensity. It can also be observed in psychologists of religion; we have been fascinated by religious motivation—such as intrinsic, extrinsic, and quest (Batson & Schoenrode, 1991; Gorsuch & McPherson, 1989)—while ignoring beliefs about the nature of reality. Unless this is understood, spirituality may misunderstand what psychology actually says about spiritual issues.

Any analysis that ignores spiritual beliefs can only be reductionistic. For example, Christianity has always held that it is what one believes is true about Jesus that is crucial. Did he live and die on a cross? Was he the Son of God? Motivation is also important, but it has to be motivation based on a belief in the validity of statements made by and about Jesus. Any psychology that does not take beliefs about the nature of reality seriously can only consider spirituality from a reductionist viewpoint.

Psychology of religion has long used the intrinsic–extrinsic (I/E) dimension as a key variable. Intrinsic is being spiritual for the sake of the spiritual itself and extrinsic is appearing spiritual only in order to gain something external to the spirituality itself, such as better health or friends. The I/E religious motivation scales began as religious "orientation" scales (Allport & Ross, 1967). While principally measuring motivation, they included some items that seemed more belief and behavior in a miscellaneous collection that was thereby limited theoretically. Gorsuch and McPherson (1989) rewrote the scales to reduce this problem, but it was best fit to a Christian worldview. We are now engaged in a rewrite of the scale so that it is more applicable to all religions, under the hypothesis that people can be intrinsically committed to other faiths than just American Protestantism (Gorsuch, Friesen, & Robert, 1998). Of course, this follows the typical psychological approach of being concerned about motivations for spirituality but not concerned for the reality toward which that spirituality is directed.

Our studies have gone beyond just the I/E motivation scales to include beliefs. We have found that the object of one's intrinsic commitment is important along with the strength of that commitment. Snook and Gorsuch (1985) examined intrinsic commitment to the Afrikaans or English versions of Christianity that existed in South Africa while the government was solely white. As predicted, the more internal the commitments in the English students, the more they wanted to include Blacks in the nation and government. Also as predicted, the more internal the commitments of Afrikaners, the more they wanted to exclude Blacks from the government. The correlations were opposite in sign! These results only make sense when one realizes the differences in beliefs between the two groups. The Afrikaners believed that God had given them the land and that they had promised to hold it for God's people. The English believed that the land was for all people (we have found beliefs important in several other studies as well).

One reason I have developed the belief–affect–value variant of reasoned action planned behavior models (Gorsuch, 1986; Schaefer & Gorsuch, 1992; Wakeman & Gorsuch, 1991; Ortberg, Gorsuch, & Kim, 2001) is that it has an explicit place for beliefs. They may be beliefs about consequences of actions, but they are based on beliefs about the world in which we live and our relationship to it.

A person's beliefs about what are likely to be the consequences of his or her actions is important in a reasoned action model. This means it is a nonreductionistic model, for the nature of one's beliefs are assumed to be influential, as well as affect (attitudes, feelings) and values. To be of use to spirituality, any psychological model must have a place for beliefs as well as motivation.

Descriptions of a Current Situation

As noted often, psychology is better at describing what currently is than at identifying what should be. That is a useful tool for spirituality. Whenever a question arises about how spirituality develops or how we should assess a current development, the descriptive facts of the situation are needed before any further assessment can be given.

I was asked to do a descriptive study of what people would want in a new hymnal. I designed a survey, analyzed it, and met with the hymnal committee at great length so they could absorb the results and what those results meant for the new hymnal. The new hymnal was sufficiently successful that I and committee members did not receive our complementary copies for over a year after it was published. They sold too fast.

We have analyzed beliefs on several occasions to see if they were related to areas of active discussion in Christian circles. One of these examined the impact of beliefs on attitudes toward homosexuals and another on attitudes toward women ministers.

In Fulton, Gorsuch, and Maynard (1999) on homosexuality and Christianity, the role of belief was examined. We predicted that the more a person believed God had dictated the Bible, the more they would judge the issue of homosexuality solely based on the Bible's (to them, God's) words. Fundamentalists—used as a descriptive term rather than a pejorative term—hold that the Bible is inerrant, with every word coming directly from God. The Bible contains lists of sins. Homosexual practices are explicitly named in those lists. For example, 1 Timothy 1:11 includes "immoral persons, sodomites, kidnappers, liars, perjurers." So the fundamentalists' position is clear: When God has said homosexuality is a sin, how can people do otherwise? The degree of fundamentalism was found to correlate with the degree of antihomosexuality. But in like manner, the more fundamentalist the student, the more they were critical of others on those New Testament lists of sinners, and even more rejecting of bigots than of homosexuals (yes, this means that those who least accepted the Bible as containing the words of God were least rejecting of bigots). This study found the religious beliefs about the Bible to be a crucial issue for homosexuality attitudes.

Hao's (1993) dissertation investigated why people hesitated to hire women pastors. One theory is that fundamentalism leads to stressing the Biblical passages that can be interpreted to support male supremacy. However, her study found that was not the case. Unlike homosexuality, fundamentalist beliefs in the Bible were unimportant. Instead the determining factor was whether they expected both current and prospective members to react negatively, so that a woman would handicap the congregation. Biblical quotes seemed to be rationalizations from that fear.

These two examples show the power of modern research to pinpoint issues that need to be addressed. Obviously, the psychology of accepting homosexuals is radically different from that of accepting women as ministers. Other examples of descriptive information about religious and spiritual topics can be found in such journals as the *Journal for the Scientific Study of Religion* and *Review of Religious Research*.

How can modern research be used to affect integration? As defined in this book, integration requires an active dialogue between two disciplines. Simply using the results of one discipline by another is fine, but it requires no dialogue between disciplines. We have long rejoiced in the value of cars to ease pastoral work, but that doesn't require integrative dialogue with physicists, automotive engineers, or mechanics. What is done with such studies is probably more central to integration than doing the studies.

The hymnal project noted previously may help to illustrate integration. I did the research because other experiences have convinced me that commercial research groups, with an occasional exception such as Search Institute's Lilly Grants and Gallup, do poor-quality research. They give businesses what the businesspeople can understand, and they are often ignorant of even relevant social science developments. They provide no professional assistance, just data collection and tabulation. In the terms of this book, there is a service bought but there is no integration.

In the hymnal project the hymnal committee and I developed the data-collection procedures together in dialogue as to the information needed for the decisions to be made. My psychology of religion knowledge (and pastoral experience) enabled a more integrative project with theological, pastoral, and psychological understandings of the results. The fact that we all shared the same denominational tradition also produced ease of communication. Some of that task involved integration because there was direct impact from both the spiritual and psychological sides.

When spirituality wishes an integrative dialogue with psychology, the prime question is one of whom to involve. To even frame the questions about what the important issues are requires due consideration of the worldviews of those who might be asked to participate. Since we are considering a spiritually based integrative effort, the worldviews of those initiating the task is a given. Then the question is that of finding psychologists who qualify on two levels. On the one hand, they must be sophisticated enough to dialogue with those from spirituality areas. On the other hand, they must know the relevant area of psychology well. Despite the most sincere intentions of dedicated Christian psychologists, none of us is qualified as a "general psychologist." The field is too big. Indeed, it is difficult for any one psychologist to even be able to recommend a knowledgeable person in all areas of psychology. So networking is necessary to find someone with appropriate psychological credentials. The appropriate credentials generally include some publications in the area.

One case of psychologists operating outside of their areas is the widespread use of clinical psychologists as general consultants in psychology. They are asked to address topics ranging from childcare to personnel selection to resolving conflicts. There are obviously a number of clinical psychologists well prepared to address one or more of these issues, but developmental, industrial–organizational, and social psychologists have direct expertise in these areas. Addressing such topics is not intrinsic to clinical psychologists' training; it is an additional competency that some develop.

Clinical psychologists are trained to help dysfunctional people become more functional. However, spirituality is for functional people growing in spirituality. Dysfunctional people, we have found, do not necessarily have much in common with functional people, which is why we need specially trained clinical psychologists with their hundreds of hours of supervised experience working with dysfunctional people. (If we could relate to dysfunctional people just as we do functional people, most of that training would not be necessary. The lack of training of lay counselors who are nevertheless successful probably lies in the mildness of the problems they confront.) The result is that clinical psychologists are trained to look for dysfunctionality in interpersonal relationships. The problem is that when it comes to normal people, there is a natural tendency to read the situation assuming dysfunctionality. This is, for example, an interpretation of the high divorce rates among clinical psychologists. They may be inclined to pathologize even normal situations and to interpret their relationship with their spouses as dysfunctional when they may actually be normal.

We do have some clinical psychologists with special expertise in working with normal people. For example, the Hunts (e.g., Hunt & Hunt, 1994) have conducted research on stability of normal marriages and have developed Methodist premarital counseling programs, and Hart (1998) has studied sexuality in highly functional men and women. Note that for both the Hunts and Hart their expertise arises from their research with normal people, not their clinical psychology. Experts such as these are able to distinguish dysfunctional and functional, but only some clinical psychologists have such broader expertise.

Although a specialist is needed, the psychologist should have some general credentials rather than be restricted to only one topic. If, for example, they had only published research on moral stages, every spirituality question will then be filtered through that perspective. Since many moral-stage researchers consider the higher stages to be better, they might not have the perspective of Jesus, who admonished us to become more childlike in our faith (Matthew 18:1–4). So, they must know the most relevant specialty in depth but also know enough general psychology to keep the specialty in perspective.

In addition to being psychology qualified, the psychologist must also be qualified in understanding the spirituality question. This does not mean that the psychologist must be a member of the same denomination or even the same religion. It does mean that the spirituality question must be understood in its ramifications. Without such an understanding, the psychologist is just hired to do a task selected by those raising the question, which is good but is also an example of use of one discipline by another discipline rather than integration. Integration arises from dialogue between disciplines. Without some experience with spirituality, a psychologist would find it difficult to have an in-depth dialogue on that subject.

Sometimes there is no psychologist available who understands the most relevant psychological domain and the nature of the spirituality questions being raised. In that case it is better to select a psychologist who clearly understands the spiritual problem at hand. Psychologists competent in any area can be expected to have several characteristics that enable them to be helpful. They know how to do literature searches and how seriously to take various results. They know how to separate the worldviews of the psychological articles from the science and can apply the latter as needed to the question at hand. They also generally have broad theories of psychology into which a set of research studies can be incorporated. But do note that a nonspecialist psychologist will need time to gain a good knowledge of the relevant psychology.

Developing Interventions to Enhance Spirituality

A major goal of spirituality–psychology integration is to help people become more spiritual. To develop such interventions, we will discuss some theory for doing so and then provide a simple example.

In addition to providing descriptive information, psychology is able to develop change programs to enhance spirituality. The spirituality defines the goals and the psychology lays out methods to achieve those goals, with an active dialogue on goal definition.

Methods are not value free, nor does spirituality say the ends justify the means. Therefore, the methods themselves should be subject to the values of spirituality. A continued dialogue between spirituality and psychology is needed to accomplish this.

To develop or fine tune interventions will require pilot projects that, following the best cannons of research methods, include control groups. The ethics of research require that no program be used unless it has been properly tested. This is one instance where some would hold that the values of spirituality differ from those of science. The primary issue seems to be the requiring of randomly assigned control groups. After all, do we not wish everyone to benefit from a spirituality-enhancement intervention?

The question of research ethics hinges on the question of human fallibility. It acknowledges that our theories are insufficient unless they are supported by data. Assuming our ideas are true is dangerous, for not all interventions are helpful, as noted in Exhibit 4.5.

Exhibit 4.5
Should All Interventions Be
Tested before Implementation?

Before World War II an intervention was funded to prevent delinquency in boys in an eastern city. The program sounded great, and would be what many would suggest even today. For each boy there was a case manager to help the boy directly and by bringing in other resources. The help included academic tutoring, medical and psychological help, and a visiting home nurse, as needed. (People who hear the description feel it would be funded today).

Stroud (1973) did a thirty-year follow-up. She found that the men who had been in the program gave strong testimony in favor of it. It played a major role in their stories of how they kept from becoming delinquent. Based on these reports alone, it would be widely recommended.

In addition to the men's stories, Stroud had other data. This came in part from the boys in the control group in the original study, for they had taken two boys from the same neighborhood block and randomly assigned one boy to the program and the other as an untreated control. Stroud interviewed the controls as well. Here are the results:

Experimental Group	Control Group
Same first arrest records	
More serious second arrests	Less serious second arrests
More blue collar jobs	More middle-class jobs
More dissatisfied with life	More happy with life
Fewer still alive	More still alive

No, the headings in the list are not reversed. Except for the personal stories, all the data show that the intervention did serious harm.

Commentary: Would you rather your child was in the experimental or control group?

If spiritually committed people without research training had done the intervention, there would have been no control group. Is that best? What would the stories alone have produced?

In research ethics, even secular psychologists are more convinced of human fallibility than those proposing spirituality programs without control groups. All spirituality interventions could produce the results of the delinquency-prevention program in Exhibit 4.5.

EXERCISE

Consider a spiritual program in which you have recently participated. Perhaps it was a set of meditations, a retreat, or a group discussion. In addition to what the participants thought it did for them, what other criteria could be used to evaluate it?

Check with those who introduced the program. What evidence can they provide that it helps? Is there data in addition to people's stories that showed it helped?

Unfortunately, most spirituality programs treat everyone as "human guinea pigs," trying out new programs without testing them for negative side effects. They fail to have a control group and fail to collect more data than just personal stories and self-report questionnaires. We just might find that some of the lack of spiritual development during our generation has been because "spirituality programs have shot themselves in the foot" with programs that only look good, or even give programs, like in Exhibit 4.5, that actually do more harm than good.

Ideally, we would like to test a new intervention carefully and yet not keep anyone from being helped. To achieve this goal I have suggested a design not found in regular research texts. It starts by dividing the participants randomly into an intervention and a control group, just as in a traditional experiment. Then, after the intervention is given to the control group and the effects measured, it adds another step. Those who were in the control group are then given the intervention. No one goes untreated and it meets the objections based on some not receiving the benefit of the intervention. (It also has some methodological advantages, such as two tests of the intervention, one comparing the control and intervention groups and a second comparing the intervention phase of the second group against its control phase.) It has a further advantage: If a negative effect is found for the intervention group, the intervention for the control group is canceled and an attempt is made to undo the damage to the intervention group. While this would not protect against delayed negative effects, it would be a step in the right direction.

As to the ethics of changing someone's spirituality, that has never been an issue for contemporary Christian spirituality. No one is forced to participate in such programs. Every church attempts to change its members spirituality every Sunday, and they proclaim that fact to the world. Everyone decides for himself or herself if he or she wishes to be exposed to that program. What would we think of a church camp that did not attempt to help children grow spiritually? Parents give their consent by the act of sending children to that camp. The fact that we become systematic about the intervention does not change the ethics of it, except to improve them by checking for negative side effects. Informed consent of participants is assumed in their choice to participate or not participate.

Can psychology be of help? Consider Exhibit 4.6.

EXHIBIT 4.6
Can an Intervention Be Effective?

Ortberg, Gorsuch, and Kim (2001) report a church-based intervention to encourage church members to donate blood at a church-sponsored blood drive. Using the belief–affect–value reasoned action model, previous research, and some pilot data, we identified beliefs, affects, and values that might be changed.

There was a wrong belief. Some thought a blood donor could catch a disease from a sick person.

There was negative affect to donating blood. Some were scared of the pain of the needle used to draw the blood.

There was a possible value problem, in that some did not see blood donating as a spirituality issue.

Interventions attended to all three areas. They were used in several Sunday classes and we just gave a standard announcement in other classes (as a control).

Here are some sample interventions:

* For changing beliefs, we noted that disease could only pass with the blood, and "so a sick person can catch a disease from you but not vice versa."

* For changing the fear of a needle, we used a desensitization procedure. "Pinch yourself. Pinch yourself again. The needle hurts no more than a pinch. Pinch yourself again. You can take pinching yourself, so you can take the needle." I assume this was ethical since they did not have to do it, but there must have been some black and blue marks the next day!

* For increasing the value of donating blood, we made an analogy to show the spiritual relevance of blood donations for Christians. "Even as Christ shed his blood for our spiritual life, we can share our blood for someone else's physical life." "Giving blood witnesses to others our Christian love."

* The results can be summarized simply. In the classes with just the standard announcement, 0 to 4 percent donated blood. In the intervention groups, 13 to 48 percent gave blood.

How, then, are the interventions to be developed? From the best psychology and the best ethics and the best spirituality, in dialogue with each other.

Integration can work.

PART III

INTEGRATION AS JOINT PROBLEM SOLVING

In Part I, the first chapter defined the task of integrating psychology and spirituality. The basic relationships among the disciplines were explored in Chapter 2. Part II developed examples of the first type of integration identified in Chapter 1, in which one discipline reflects upon another. The second type of integration is Joint Problem Solving. That is the subject of Part III.

Joint Problem Solving is on a continuum of what this project has defined as complete integration—when both spirituality and psychological disciplines are involved—to no integration, as in when one discipline uses standard information from another. Integrating is not always necessary or desirable. It cannot be judged more desirable than no integration unless the situation warrants it. Spiritual situations should not be psychologized and psychological situations should not be spiritaulized just to make them fit our notion of integration. (Note that formally exploring Joint Problem Solving Integration is so new that I have only a notion of what this paragraph means in action. Experience, dialogue, and research are needed to explore these issues. As suggested by Heather Brikett Cattell [personal communication, 27 November 1998], case studies would be most useful to further clarify such issues. Hopefully the years ahead will provide some.)

Clinical psychology has been the primary focus for integration to date, and is the topic of Chapter 5. Chapter 6 then develops joint problem solving in the area of social psychology. Obviously, there are other areas of psychology that could form the basis for joint problem solving, such as developmental (e.g., Steele, 1986) or personality (e.g., McDonald, 1986). Vande Kemp (1998) has called for an integration that draws from and informs "all domains of general psychology" (p. 202); that touches a very responsive cord in this writer, but is the task for another book. These two areas were selected because of the extent of literature, the needs in clinical psychology, and the potential for social psychology with which I am acquainted.

Joint Problem Solving Integration could be organized around spiritual topics rather than psychological topics. These might include chapters such as "search for meaning," "social support and pastoral care," "surrendering to God," or the twelve-step program's reliance on "a higher power." McMinn (1996) follows this approach, and Faw (1995) is similar. The psychological organization was selected for one reason: Psychology is my primary area of expertise.

Integration as Joint Problem Solving is still in its first generation as far as effective dialogue is concerned. Perhaps these chapters will stimulate more of it.

CHAPTER 5

Clinical Psychology

Clinical psychology has been the major area for integration discussions in recent years. That is, of course, because clinical psychology treats people with problems, and these often involve explicitly religious issues. Indeed, clinical psychology as much or more than any other part of psychology is integrative by nature (Browning, 1987). What problems addressed by clinical psychology could avoid areas of spirituality involving values and ethics? These issues need to be addressed (Bergin, 1991).

There are numerous excellent books in this area, including those in Exhibit 5.1. Apropos the previous paragraph, Payne, Bergin, and Loftus (1992) discuss how values and the patient's religious practices could be included in therapy. Many of the books are Christian—and some very conservative—because Christians have been highly interested in the integration discussions in clinical psychology.

EXHIBIT 5.1
Books on the Integration of
Spirituality and Clinical Psychology

Browning, D. S. (1987). *Religious Thought and the Modern Psychologies.* Philadelphia: Fortress.

Collins, G. (1980). *Christian counseling: A comprehensive guide.* Waco, TX: Word.

Cosgrove, M., & Mallory, J. (1977). *Mental health: A Christian perspective.* Grand Rapids, MI: Zondervan.

Crabb, L. J., Jr. (1977). *Effective biblical counseling: A model of helping caring Christians become capable counselors.* Grand Rapids, MI: Zondervan.

Dueck, A. C. (1995). *Between Jerusalem and Athens.* Grand Rapids, MI: Baker Books.

Ellison, C. (1994). *From stress to well-being.* Dallas, TX: Word.

Hurding, R. (1992). *The Bible and counseling.* London: Hodder and Stoughton.

Jones, S. L., & Buttman, R. E. (1991). *Modern psychotherapies: A comprehensive Christian appraisal.* Downers Grove, IL: Intervarsity Press.

Lovinger, R. J. (1984). *Working with religious issues in therapy.* New York: Jason Aronson.

Lovinger, R. J. (1990). *Religion and counseling: The psychological impact of religious belief.* New York: Continuum.

Malony, H. N. (1983). *Wholeness and holiness: Readings in the psychology and theology of mental health.* Grand Rapids, MI: Baker.

McLemore, C. (1982). *The scandal of psychotherapy.* Wheaton, IL: Tyndale.

McMinn, M. R. (1996) *Psychology, theology, and spirituality in Chrisitian counseling.* Wheaton, IL: Tyndale House.

Meier, P., Minirth, F., Wichern, F., & Ratcliff, D. (1991). *Introduction to psychology and counseling.* Grand Rapids, MI: Baker.

Miller, W. R. (Ed.). (1999). *Integrating spirituality into treatment.* Washington, DC: American Psychological Association.

Miller, W. R., & Martins, J. E. (Eds.). (1988). *Behavior therapy and religion: Integrating spiritual and behavioral approaches to change.* Newbury Park, CA: Sage.

Richards, P. S., & Bergin, A. E. (Eds.). (1997). *A spiritual strategy for counseling and pyschotherapy.* Washington, DC: American Psychological Association.

Sanders, R. K. (Ed.). (1997). *Christian counseling ethics: A handbook for therapists, pastors, & counselors.* Downers Grove, IL: InterVarsity Press.

Shafranske, E. P. (Ed.). (1996). *Religion and the clinical practice of psychology.* Washington, DC: American Psychological Association.

Southard, S. (1972). *Christians and mental health.* Nashville: Broadman.

Southard, S. (1989). *Theology and therapy.* Dallas, TX: Word.

Stern, E. M. (Ed.). (1985). *Psychotherapy and the religiously committed patient.* New York: Hayworth.

Tan, S.-Y. (1991). *Lay counseling: Equipping Christians for a helping ministry.* Grand Rapids, MI: Zondervan.

Tjeltveit, A. (1999). *Ethics and values in psychotherapy.* New York: Routledge.

Worthington, E. L. (Ed.). (1993). *Psychotherapy and religious values.* Grand Rapids, MI: Baker.

The definitions of Chapter 1 for this project are not used in many of the references. They have their own definitions of integration. Moreover, what clinicians may refer to as integration may have little to do with any more formal development. That is not to say one usage is better than another, but instead we can continue to expect the term "integration" to have multiple usages. So pay close attention to what meaning, implicitly if not explicitly, an author uses. Some of the clinical psychology discussions in Exhibit 5.1 are good examples of Commentary Integration, one discipline reflecting on another. Others are Joint Problem Solving Integration, but for many it is difficult to place them clearly in either type. Moreover, parts of the discussions referenced in Exhibit 5.1 are not integration as the term is used in this project but, instead, are aspects of either psychology or spirituality that may be useful. But just because it doesn't neatly fit in a type or it is questionable if it truly is integration by this project's definition does not mean it is unimportant. Many of the more important issues in clinical psychology are clearly a matter of spirituality and ethics or clearly a matter of psychology. These must be understood as a prerequisite for integration in the sense it is discussed here.

While categories such as these two types of integration are a useful tool, too rigid a use of them would assume that there are no borderline cases. That would distort the complex nature of clinical psychology itself. You will note that this chapter's material ranges from clear cases of integration to borderline cases, and that some cannot be classified neatly. But that's fine; they still need to be discussed.

As Tan (1996) notes, clinical psychology integration varies from implicit to explicit. Implicit is when it forms a background and a context in which the therapy is based but is not mentioned in the therapy session per se. Explicit is when spirituality is a focus in the therapy itself, whether through topics in the discussion or the use of spiritual resources such as meditation or prayer. By these definitions the sections vary on the continuum from clearly implicit to possibly explicit, depending on how the issues are resolved and manifest themselves.

GOAL: THE ENHANCEMENT OF SELF-ESTEEM?

A basic point of integration is to ask what the goal for clinical psychology is from psychology's and spirituality's perspectives. There is considerable common ground in defining problems, such as psychosis, neurological problems, and many neurotic problems. These are all deficit problems, where the people are clearly handicapped so that they are not able to achieve goals. Such deficit problems involve minor spirituality integration, for the individuals cannot achieve any goals effectively, including spiritual goals, until the deficit is removed.

Note that many outpatient clients do not have clear deficits of the type of the previous paragraph. Instead, clients are unhappy, depressed, or unfulfilled. No psychosis is involved, neither have they lost capabilities due to injury. Indeed, to casual observers the client seems to be doing well. But that is not the client's own judgment. What then is the goal of therapy? The point of integrative discussion about goals of therapy is to identify the goals once basic deficits are resolved.

Psychology has the tradition of considering the goal of therapy to be the person's own happiness. But if the client knew what would make him or her happy and how to achieve it, there would be no need for a therapist. Therefore, the question is more than just whether the client is happy.

Bergin and Payne (1991) note that the goals of psychotherapy beyond deficit correction may, for a particular psychologist, be an unexamined assumption that the therapist can minimize the impact of moral values or can just use the standard ones of the culture. However, "The danger of a moral philosophy or moral frame of reference not anchored to spirituality or religion is that of relativeness, expediency, and an ever-changing hierarchy of values" (p. 201). Integration requires that spirituality be involved in all such discussions of goals of therapy.

At this point, traditional psychology and Christianity have different emphases. Two are particularly notable. First is the individualism of traditional psychology. The client is the only one the therapist sees. Knowledge of the situation and the role of others are only seen through the client's eyes. In addition, the client's happiness is the only happiness considered.

This individualism in traditional psychology is natural, since psychology studies each person. However, it is not particularly modern psychology. The last few decades have often found that it is the person in a social situation who is most understandable. No person exists outside of a social context.

Christian spirituality is supportive of an individual but within a group focus. The individual is recognized as central to spirituality. The New Testament consistently challenges the individual to grow in his or her relationship to God. It clearly recognizes the individual as the unit of ethical responsibility and decision making. However, spirituality also has very strong interpersonal focuses, at least in the Christian faith. The New Testament challenges to which we just referred are generally challenges not only of commitment to God but of commitment to others as well. The story of the Good Samaritan (Luke 10:29–37) is a story of personal decision making as to who is one's neighbor. That decision making impacts the neighbor, and the story would be pointless without that interpersonal dimension. Nor would it be possible to understand Jesus without understanding the Jewish culture of his time. As if this were not enough, the two millennia of Christianity have been two millennia of individual Christians within a church context. A Christian without the interpersonal context of the church is almost a contradiction in terms.

The integration of clinical psychology and Christian spirituality would not deny the individual focus but would rather suggest expansion of that focus to reach out to others. "With whom shall this person be?" is an issue that spirituality would suggest needs to be a question as much as "Whom shall this person be?" To have one without the other is to have an incomplete person. This, then, is not a radical redefinition of therapy but rather developing an integrative focus that, in keeping with classical psychology, begins with the individual and then, in keeping with Christian spirituality, ends with the person's interpersonal impact.

The integration just noted might necessitate some changes in perspective regarding marital therapy. When a person with a problem marriage is seen in classical psychotherapy, the quickest way to help the person become happier may well be divorce. However, the spirituality-informed psychologist would need to ask about the impact on the rest of the client's family. A systems- or family-oriented therapy model may be best for spiritually informed marriage therapy.

In addition to the interpersonal focus that Christian spirituality emphasizes more than traditional psychology, there is a second difference in emphasis. The second difference is on the evaluation of the self. Clinical psychology has placed a strong emphasis on self-esteem; that is, the value that individual clients place on themselves. Classical psychological therapy has had a major goal of increasing clients' self-esteem.

Christian spirituality looks at self-esteem differently than psychology (Vitz, 1977; Adams, 1986). The emphasis is not that people should value themselves highly, but the opposite. Truly spiritual people realize that they are far from perfection. They are so far from perfection that the idea that God loves them is difficult to accept, for we are unworthy of that love. Further, we are weak and cannot obtain that perfect level that would maximize our self-esteem and warrant God's love. Instead, we are encouraged to accept God's forgiveness in repentance and be servants of others. It is inappropriate that that we might even ask to "sit on the Lord's right or left hand" and thus be a recognized leader, but it is very appropriate for us to "wash other people's feet" (John 13:12–16). Humility is the hallmark of a Christian spiritual person.

The difference of view between Christians and psychologists has led to problems with the operational definition of Maslow's self-actualization, the Personal Orientation Inventory (Wulff, 1997, p. 695). In addition to some clearly antireligious items (Garner & Garfinkel, 1997, p. 200), Garner points out that "restraint of impulse" and "self-sacrifice" lowers scores on this instrument. But both are seen as spiritually desirable in Christianity.

How can Christianity and psychology be so far apart if psychology is simply exploring how God has made us? The valuing of one's own judgment over that of God is identified as the source of estrangement from God. Eve and Adam decided their decision about eating the fruit in the Garden of Eden would be better than God's (Genesis 3:1–13). They obviously had great faith in their judgment and so must have had high self-esteem. This resulted in what Christian theology refers to as the "fall from grace." It is a result of placing ourselves higher than God, which happens when we place our self-esteem as the prime goal.

There are several lines of reasoning within psychology that are finding results more compatible with spirituality's view of self-esteem than psychology's, and that may serve as a corrective to overreliance on high self-esteem. We saw previously that human judgment is quite limited, and an area for humility rather than pride. To the degree that high self-esteem means that we feel our judgments are excellent when they really aren't, we are ignoring our psychological knowledge of the lack of perfection in our decision making. Such overvaluing of decisions probably underlies the phrase "Pride goes before a fall," for we overestimate the quality of our decisions, and then find out the truth.

A line of reasoning within psychology that counters the image of high self-esteem being appropriate is found in Baumeister's (1997) book on evil. His summary of research on self-esteem suggests a new phrase: "Pride goes before hurting others." That research found that people who hurt others were higher in self-esteem than less-violent people. In Baumeister's conclusions he indicates "threatened ego" is one of the four sources of evil. By "threatened ego" he means that someone else does not place as high a value on us as we do, and that encourages us to become forceful to the point of violence to convince him or her otherwise. Not only are individuals with high self-esteem more likely to hurt others, he traces how the increase of a group's self-esteem over time tracks with an increase in the violence of that group toward outsiders.

With spiritual evaluations of psychology suggesting that psychology finds, on the one hand, that part of us created in the image of God and also, on the other hand, that part of us showing our fallen state, psychology is coming closer to agreement with Christian spirituality. Given Baumeister's findings, high self-esteem can no longer be said to be an unconditional good. Instead, it appears to be more a part of our fallen state than our image of God. As more research accumulates, psychology comes closer to the conclusion of spirituality that humility is characteristic of the spiritual person. Hence, we are seeing a convergence.

Note that Christian spirituality does not encourage self-esteem per se, but it does encourage acceptance of ourselves as we are. "While we were yet sinners Christ died for us" (Romans 5:8) is one of the many passages in the New Testament affirming that God loves us unconditionally. We do not have to be perfect (which is good, since with our limited reasoning powers we have no chance of being perfect). That acceptance of ourselves has probably been mistakenly identified as self-esteem in psychological literature.

May it be that we can accept others with their faults only if we accept ourselves with our faults? Self-acceptance—"warts and all"— seems more appropriate for us than high self-esteem.

There are other suggestions from spirituality for consideration when setting goals in clinical psychology. Exhibit 5.2 suggests that what would seem a universally good goal, lowering anxiety, may need to be judged from the ethical context of the situation, and thus be integrated with spirituality.

EXHIBIT 5.2
When Is Low Anxiety Best?

If we found a person with high anxiety, we would be naturally concerned. A goal of therapy would be to lower that anxiety. But what about the following cases?

- Person A, with snake phobia, refuses to carry out a job due to anxiety about being bitten by a snake. Situation: His boss told him to clean out an outbuilding where the last two people who had tried to clean it were in the hospital for poisonous snake bites. Inappropriate intervention: Desensitization to remove fear of snakes. Appropriate interventions: (1) Assertiveness (aggressiveness?) training so client throws the boss in the building before entering, (2) hiring a snake professional to clean the building, or (3) the therapist cleaning the snakes out of the building. The client will then be able to function effectively in the building without a snake phobia.

- Person B has reoccurring anxiety attacks about falling on concrete and being injured. Situation: In training for parachute jumping. Inappropriate intervention: Progressive desensitization so that they view falling on concrete as painless (possibly by first from five feet, then six feet, then seven feet, and so on). Appropriate intervention: Referral to a specialist to teach the person how to minimize injury when landing.

- Person C is afraid of being attacked by vicious beasts. Situation: Living in Rome during the time when Christians were literally thrown to the lions. Appropriate interventions: Teach them to live with the anxiety, lessen the anxiety by strengthening their Christianity so martyrdom is greeted with rejoicing rather than anxiety, or eliminate the practice of people being killed for entertainment.

Commentary: The first two examples remind us that clinical goals are best understood in a situational context, with which all sensible psychologists agree. The third example illustrates that different worldviews may lead to different decisions. Some spiritually sound decisions may increase rather than decrease anxiety.

EXERCISE

Try writing an even better illustration to substitute for one of the first two in Exhibit 5.2, and for the third. When, depending on your view of spirituality, should someone be highly anxious or depressed if he or she is truly spiritual?

A decade or so ago I mentioned in my research classes that there was a scale available for almost anything one wanted to measure. Then a student asked about forgiveness, and that student was right. There was neither scale nor research program in that area. Since then, Susan Wade (1989) and Judy Hao (Hao & Gorsuch, 1993) at Fuller have investigated the area. Mike McCullough (an intern at Fuller at about that time) is centering a research program on forgiveness, with coauthors such as Worthington (e.g., McCullough, Worthington, & Rachal, 1997). Enright is also active in the area with associates (e.g., Enright & the Human Development Group, 1996). The area is rapidly growing and still young, so that almost any statement about it as an area would be dated by the time it was published (but do check Meek & McMinn, 1997). Nevertheless, it is mentioned here for two reasons. First, it is a criterion for therapy that comes out of one spirituality tradition, and hopefully will be a model for other traditions that may also come from spirituality. Second, forgiveness holds considerable potential for a clinical psychology that is willing to recognize that interpersonal relationships are as important as an individual's self-concepts. Christian spirituality's emphasis on forgiveness is becoming established as a concern for at least Christian clinical psychologists. However, we must recognize that not all spiritual traditions emphasize forgiveness of enemies to the degree that Christians do.

Evaluating the criteria for positive mental health is an area for active integration. Positive mental health goals are in part obvious to all people, such as happiness, but there are other goals that may differ depending on worldviews. Restitution and punishment of the guilty party might be considered better than forgiveness. The orientation toward positive self-regard might change as a function of spirituality. Once goals are identified, social science research can evaluate if more spiritual or religious people have positive mental health.

Writers have counted studies to see the benefits of being religious (e.g., Batson & Ventis, 1993; Hood, Spilka, Hunsberger, & Gorsuch, 1996; Payne, Bergin, Bielema, & Jenkins, 1991) and generally conclude that, in our culture, religious people are less anxious and less likely to be a problem socially (e.g., less abuse of substances [Gorsuch, 1995]). Since these have turned out positive, culture and Christianity agree.

But what if the studies had turned out negative, with the more religious showing less mental health? Three interpretations would be possible. On the one hand, a conclusion might be that religion is bad for us. In fact, Batson (1976) has long asked, "Is religion on our side?" and is doubtful. On the other hand, the criteria for mental health might not match the goals of spirituality. On the third hand (if you are a Mote, Hindu god, or other creature with more than two hands [Niven & Pournelle, 1993]; otherwise substitute "on the first foot"), the conclusion may be that the culture is bad for us, since it does not provide the environment that enhances Christian spirituality. So if the results are negative in some area, we cannot decide whether the people, the research, or the culture should change until there is integration with spirituality.

DIFFERENCES BETWEEN CLINICAL PSYCHOLOGY
AND PASTORAL MINISTRY

Integration of clinical psychology and spirituality occurs because of shared interests in helping people. Each has a separate tradition of providing such help. For psychology it is clinical and counseling psychology. For spirituality it has been, for the example of Christianity, the church and pastoral ministry. Both of these disciplines seek to help people through hard times. They are also united in their faith that people can be helped.

To describe the relationship of psychologists with ministers, psychologists have used the "gatekeeper" model. In this model, much is made of the fact that ministers are, for religious people, often the first people they turn to when they have problems. A minister then has the option of working with the person or referring him or her to a clinical psychologist. It seems that psychologists have often considered ministers only in this sense, simply as people to refer clients to them.

The gatekeeper model has several limitations (Gorsuch & Meylink, 1988; Meylink & Gorsuch, 1986a, 1986b, 1988). The first limitation is a pragmatic one. All the benefits go to the psychologist and none to the minister. Even ministers who often refer to psychologists complain about the lack of reciprocity. A second problem is the lack of feedback to ministers on referrals that they make. I am not, of course, suggesting that confidences be violated. I am rather suggesting some feedback is necessary, if only to say that there were a certain number of meetings and both the therapist and client thought it successful (with permission from the client as appropriate). Without such feedback the minister is left ignorant of the information needed to decide whether future referrals to this psychologist are warranted. Blind referrals, that is, referrals when you are unsure of the help that might be provided, are unethical.

With two professions both wishing to help people with problems, it is important to recognize appropriate divisions of labor. These divisions arise from the different assumptions on which pastoral ministering and clinical psychology are based.

Exhibit 5.3 shows the results of Leung's (1991) master's level project. It is based upon expert judgment as to which type of problem should be sent to what kind of professional for help. The judges were people with both clinical psychology and ministerial graduate training and experience. Being experienced practitioners in both areas was deemed the necessary background to identify the boundaries between these two areas.

EXHIBIT 5.3
Which Problem Goes to Which Professional?

Ministers	Psychologists
Direction in spiritual searching	Depression
Direction in life	Phobias
Understanding of Biblical truths	Anxiety disorders
Acute grief and uncomplicated mourning	Personality disorders
Minor relational and personal problems	Major relational problems, particularly marital or family problems

---

Note the distinctive emphases within each profession in Exhibit 5.3. Ministers are naturally used with problems that are solely spiritual or religious, and psychologists with problems that arise from major problems of the person. In terms of integration, these problems, as stated, are primarily in one area or the other and hence only occasionally require integration.

In discussions of Leung's (1991) results, some psychologists have debated the last two points under ministers. These probably could go to either, but cost–effectiveness considerations place them clearly on the ministry side. However, these points may go to psychologists when a person has no spiritual counselor.

It would make our task much easier if each person with an issue would place themselves clearly in one or the other of the categories in Exhibit 5.3. Unfortunately, that does not always happen. A person may not know what the problem is. A person may have multiple issues that change over time. Or the issue itself may fit several of the categories, cutting across both ministry and psychology. Then integration—the bringing together of two disciplines to jointly address the problem—will be necessary. Note that the implication is that both ministers and psychologists need to know enough about the other profession to know when and how to refer.

Does Exhibit 5.3 mean we can only choose either a minister or a psychologist to provide the help when the problem is both spiritual and psychological? Not at all. It is possible—and necessary—for all psychologists to respect and include the spiritual perspectives of their clients (see Exhibit 5.1; W. Miller, 1988).

As Meylink and Gorsuch (Gorsuch & Meylink, 1988; Meylink & Gorsuch, 1986a, 1986b, 1988) have pointed out, a coprofessional model is warranted. Coprofessional models assume that each profession has an area of specialty and expertise. Resource collaboration (Pargament, 1997) occurs as each respects the other. People are referred back and forth as needed, given their situation. Not only might a minister refer a person with a clear psychological problem to a psychologist, but a psychologist would refer a client with a clear spiritual problem to a minister. They might concurrently counsel the same person or engage in occasional cotherapy. Unless the professional is trained in both areas—that is, has graduate course work and supervised experience as a psychologist and as a minister—the minister or psychologist must be wise, first, as to the help he or she can provide and, second, as to both when and to whom referrals should be made.

Is a minister ever needed if psychologists are doing their work well? It is my impression that some psychologists feel that they can handle—or they must handle—every problem that a person brings to them (with the sole exception being if there is an actual physical problem needing a medical doctor, such as a possible brain tumor). "Anything a minister could do, a psychologist can do better." This idea may have accidentally spread more widely than it should because pastoral counseling as a specialty within ministry has often used the same methods as many psychologists.

The position that psychologists can virtually replace ministers is misleading, for most psychologists have little training in spiritual matters beyond that of the lay person (Shafranske & Gorsuch, 1984). For psychologists to be properly equipped to counsel true spiritual problems, which include most of those listed in Exhibit 5.3 under "ministers," they would need training and experience in ministry per se. That means, for most religious groups, an applied degree, such as the MDiv, followed by ordination as well as experience in ministry itself. Even in a dual-degree program involving both psychology and theology such as ours at Fuller, the emphasis is on theology rather than practical ministry. For example, Fuller Ph.D. psychology students who take a MDiv degree do not have the supervised experience usually required for ministry. They receive a waiver on that because of their psychology experience. The assumption is that they will never do ministry nor consult with a person with only a spiritual problem. But might this not mean that all psychologists who are not also ordained with appropriate practical training as ministers should refer any person whose problem is under "ministers" in Exhibit 5.3?

I slipped a new word into the last paragraph: ordained. That is important because it, along with "minister," points to several unique characteristics of the clergy in most religious traditions. First, ordination means that the spiritual tradition has examined and set the person aside for ministry. It is somewhat equivalent to the notion of state licensing; a degree alone is not sufficient for "hanging out a shingle" to practice psychology, nor is an MDiv sufficient to be recognized as a minister. In both cases representatives of the community that they will serve set procedures by which quality is assured.

Being ordained means, second, that the minister becomes a representative of God and the Church. While in my theology lay people are called to be philosophers, psychologists, physicists, and to other occupations, they are not called to be representatives of the Church in the same manner as clergy. Having been a minister for a congregation within a denomination that historically minimizes the differences between clergy and laity, I have witnessed the uniqueness of the ministry. Just the presence of an ordained minister can have a unique impact upon a person. Spiritual counseling as well as the other tasks in the "ministers" column do not have the same meaning if a psychologist attempts them. Therefore it is impossible—and always will be—for a psychologist who is not also an ordained minister to be as effective in some areas as a minister from the client's religious tradition (and it may be impossible for the psychologist who is also a minister to fulfill the ministerial role when the client sees him or her primarily as a psychologist).

A third unique aspect of ordained ministers that separates them from psychologists is that ministers are involved in a long-term relationship. They baptize, marry, and bury people within their congregations. They speak to them in worship each week and see many of them in various small groups during the week. This involvement means that they know the individuals in multiple settings and have a number of ways to help them. It also means that, unlike the psychologist, they participate with people in the normal rhythms of joy and sorrow. This ministerial involvement is unlike most psychology, in which the emphasis is on limited time interventions, which is appropriate if we assume we can help people as psychologists. The psychologist is invited by clients into their lives and then exits when the intervention is completed. (There is other therapy that is long term; my suspicion is that some psychologists prefer that because they like a long relationship with people such as ministers have. But a psychologist is not the client's minister, but only an expert to help solve a specific set of problems and then get out of their lives.)

The position that a psychologist can do whatever a minister can encourages unethical practice. It is unethical because, as the California psychology licensing law states, it is only legal and ethical for psychologists to practice in areas for which they have training and supervised experience. To my knowledge, training and supervised experience in spirituality as approached by clergy are not officially available in any current doctoral psychology program (including programs at religious institutions). Who among them has been trained to conduct funerals to help resolve grief and to counsel families during the year of grief? Who among psychologists has been at the bedside of a dozen people while they died, learning firsthand what that entails? Who has learned the variations in normal grief from working with the families of the deceased over the next year? Training to be equivalent to the minister's would need considerable time for a psychologist due to the very limited overlap between the two degrees (part of the time would be to counter the negative transfer from the practices of one profession to the other).

Spirituality, of course, includes more than just those active in an organized religion. For spiritual but nonreligious people it is hard to know to whom they can turn who would have the training and expertise that ministers have within their religious organizations. I suggest that this need for a place to turn to is one reason why most spirituality movements have been, over time, institutionalized into religious or quasi-religious organizations.

But psychologists sensitive to spirituality and religious issues should be able to help minor spiritual problems and can engage the coprofessional model. In the coprofessional model psychologists recognize their main task is not religious direction. They therefore refer clients to appropriate ministers for spiritual direction and counseling. That referral may be concurrent with the psychological therapy or may be an additional step after the therapy, or the psychologist and minister may do cotherapy. While some psychologists with special integration training may do spiritual counseling also and some ministers may be better counselors than many highly trained psychologists, they should be the exception to the rule.

The coprofessional model assumes that psychologists know appropriate ministers to whom they can refer clients. This is the same issue in any referral. Knowledge about referrals comes from psychologists seeking out appropriate ministers. This may mean interviewing several ministers as well as consulting other community resources. Naturally, psychologists must know various types of spirituality sufficiently to understand which religious tradition would have a minister compatible with that of the client.

FOR WHAT KIND OF INTEGRATION ARE OR SHOULD CLINICAL PSYCHOLOGISTS BE TRAINED?

Except in the Christian-based clinical programs such as we have at Fuller, psychologists are currently not trained at all in relating to clergy, nor do we have a database that applies to referral or other collaboration (Weaver et al., 1997). The recent books in Exhibit 5.1 suggest some interest in the interface with spirituality, but those seldom discuss interactions with clergy.

In the last section it was concluded that it is impossible for a clinical psychologist to become the client's minister in the sense of clergy, but that each clinical psychologist should contribute to the spirituality of the client to the degree that the psychologist has the appropriate training to do so. This suggests that most clinical psychologists will, because of no special development of spiritual training skills or supervised experience, be operating at a level closer to that of the average committed church person when it comes to spirituality, if they are themselves active within a spiritual tradition. But it gets worse; Sorenson (1994a, 1994b, 1997) has found that how psychologists work with spiritual issues in therapy is primarily a function of whether they have personal experiences with a clinician that does so. Hence, the lack of integration of spirituality into therapy is self-perpetuating.

The lack of integration training for clinical psychologists exists in part because the history of clinical psychology has included many who have been taught that clinical treatment is free of all spirituality and hence they need no training in this area. Bergin (1991) and Shafranske and Malony (1996), as well as most of the references in Exhibit 5.1, are among those pointing out that therapy is not value free but is embedded in worldview assumptions and spiritual commitments. In addition, earlier chapters noted that decisions always involve values. Other elements, such as beliefs about consequences and attitudes toward those consequences, are important but do not eliminate values being involved whenever human decisions are being made. Human decisions are always a part of therapy; often one purpose of therapy is to enable the client to develop better decision making for the future. Hence, therapy has involved and always will involve values, and therefore has a spiritual component.

The degree of integration with spirituality varies from one specialty to another in clinical psychology. Those doing neuropsychological assessments and those working with hospitalized psychotics would seem to need less emphasis on spirituality than other areas of psychology. While that is so, emphasis is still needed (see Boisen, 1936, for the spiritual journey of a psychotic). If the neuropsychological practice involves those whose are sick or injured, spirituality issues will be engaged. Moreover, since those working with psychotics may have occasion to work with the families of those patients, spiritual issues will arise, both with the patients and with the families.

Psychologists specializing in behavior modification with children may also need less emphasis on spirituality. This holds to the degree that the children are sufficiently young that basic socialization is the task at hand. Basic socialization—such as being honest and respecting others in groups—appears common to all cultures and spiritualities. Of course, many who start by doing only such behavior modification eventually are involved in broader issues, which again necessitates integration with spirituality.

The need for training in spirituality is clearly apparent for psychologists training to work with "walk-in" clients. They will have the full spectrum of human problems and therefore human decision making. Moreover, since therapy often proceeds in unanticipated directions, a solid foundation in spirituality is essential.

Note that the discussion has been centered on "training in spirituality" rather than "being spiritual." Even the most nonspiritual clinical psychologists need to understand some basics of spirituality in order to understand their clients. The degree of such understanding should be sufficient for the psychologist to decide when it is proper to treat the client, or when the client should be referred either to another psychologist better trained in spirituality or to a minister. Referral is desirable or essential when the spirituality of the client is one little understood by the therapist, the client is spiritually committed in a manner contrary to the therapist's commitment, or the problems are clearly spiritual issues.

EXERCISE

If you are a psychologist or minister, what are your limits in dealing with the problems of Exhibit 5.3? Can you develop a good list of professionals to whom you can refer a person? If you are in training, to what degree do those who are training you recognize their limits? What limits do you expect to have?

SPIRITUAL RESOURCES

This section addresses some of the more basic areas of spiritual resources for integration. The resources available in each major tradition of spirituality are numerous and the following just touches the surface. They are discussed in more detail in the books listed in Exhibit 5.1. For example, Miller (1999) has chapters on meditation (Marlatt & Kristeller), prayer (McCullough & Larson), twelve-step programs (Tonigan, Toscova, & Connors), values (Richards, Rector, & Tjeltveit), spiritual surrender (Cole & Pargament), acceptance and forgiveness (Sanderson & Linehan), hope (Yahne & Miller), and serenity (Connors, Toscova, & Tonigan).

Meditation

A basic spiritual resource available from almost any spirituality tradition is that of meditation. Meditation involves withdrawal from normal consciousness with an emphasis upon a form of consciousness that is tranquil compared to normal life. It may be ideational or nonideational, with the former using imagery from within the Christian or other spirituality tradition. The latter often involves exercises of a noncognitive type that help produce the altered state.

Meditation is also used to describe a devotional program with time set aside to contemplate and pray. Christians often find group worship to be a meditative experience that serves as a refocusing on the more spiritual aspects of life.

Meditation research (Hood et al., 1996, pp. 193–198) has been principally in Eastern traditions of meditation. Zen meditation clearly increases the amplitude of alpha waves in the brain. The research on the effects of meditation suggests that it can help reduce an addict's substance abuse, although the studies are limited because of dropouts. Other benefits are also claimed.

Meditation is one spirituality resource that is probably underused.

Readings

If the tradition of spirituality of the client includes printed materials, those can be quite useful. The readings might be preselected by the therapist, or the client may simply engage in a reading program of his or her own or as laid out by another, such as his or her minister. The readings may also be combined with meditation. Johnson (1992) discusses how rational–emotive therapy can use scriptures.

Christians have long reported that reading the Bible systematically, even without regard to one's own problems, has generated useful insights (and, hopefully, change). The insights gained are seldom predictable. These insights can be used in the therapy sessions or as an outside source of support for the client.

Interpreting sacred writings such as the Bible is more complex than it may initially seem. Scriptures were written in a different place and time, knowledge of which is important in going beyond the initial sense of the text. Generally, this is not a problem for religious people using scriptures for daily meditation. However, if there is a clinical issue tied up with a Biblical interpretation, then the therapist needs to know how those who have studied the text in the client's tradition understand that text (Lovinger, 1996, pp. 343–346, gives a brief overview of such issues with the Bible).

From a Christian perspective, a therapy goal is to help the client move from being self-centered to having a better balance between self and other. This task might benefit from a reading program. The readings, if appropriately selected, will lead the client toward others as much as toward himself or herself. This gives openings for the client to explore the need to relate to others and to serve them.

Religious Coping Styles

Pargament (1997) summarizes a program of research on religious coping (while it is within the Judeo–Christian tradition, the results may generalize to other traditions of spirituality). Religious coping is a paradigm with much potential for integrating spirituality into clinical psychology; I recommend Pargament's book to all clinical psychologists interested in spirituality.

Briefly, the program of research on religious coping has found several coping styles. These include Self-Directive, where the person attempts to solve the problem on their own; Deferring, where the person turns the problem completely over to God to solve; Surrendering, where the person asks God what God would have them to do and surrenders his or her own will to that (Wong-McDonald, 1999); and

Collaborative, where the person and God work together on problems. The research results are clear: Collaborative and Surrendering coping styles are related to fewer psychological problems (Bjorck, 1993; Pargament, 1997; Wong-McDonald, 1999).

Unfortunately, the research program has not yet reached the stage of documenting interventions to alter person's modes of religious coping. Hopefully a clinical psychologist knowledgeable in this research literature could direct the client toward better modes of coping.

The Religious Community

In religious spirituality traditions the religious community is a possible source of support for the client. Typically, this is considered under the category of social support, and social support is assumed to be beneficial.

How well clinical psychologists can use the religious community is a difficult question with few available resources to help. Clinical psychology has always emphasized the therapist–client interaction as the source of change. If others, such as spouses, are involved, they join the psychologist and client in a session. There is some tradition of systems work in marital and family therapy, but this too is not sufficiently oriented toward broader communities to answer the need.

Perhaps the religious community could be involved if a minister is also working with the client. That would, if it were the client's minister, give a natural entrée into the religious community. This area needs considerable more work before we know what the possibilities are.

DEMONIC SPIRITUALITY

In this book I have assumed that spirituality is good. I suspect that most readers will be from traditions of spirituality that are positive. But we must note that spirituality need not necessarily be good.

Many religious traditions contain the notion of evil or negative spirituality. These may be labeled demons or evil spirits, or it may just be the result of "wrong-thinking" spirituality. In the non-Western world the concept of active evil spirits or demons is strong. However, it also occurs in the United States; surprisingly (at least to me), the majority of people report some such belief (MacNutt, 1995). These beliefs are more common among conservative Christians who accept the New Testament description of evil spirits as authenticating them. Psychologists with clients with worldviews that include evil spirits will need to be especially alert to client's concepts of possession and spiritual healing. Possession normally is not seen in any of these traditions as a problem for psychologists, but rather as a problem for spiritual leaders to treat, in part because they have procedures to follow (see, e.g., MacNutt, 1995). People from traditions with a strong sense of negative spirituality who are exposed to Western psychology will, hopefully, develop theories and models to differentiate between possession in their worldviews and psychological problems. Such models are dependent upon worldviews and are not yet widely discussed in Western psychology or spirituality.

In most traditions spirituality is generally seen as negative when it is at obvious variance to the major thrust of that spirituality tradition. Two examples can be found in psychological research literature. Gorsuch (1995) reports that a restrictive religious upbringing—one characterized by punishment and a limiting rather than a freeing religion—is related to problems. Those treating alcoholics report many have spiritual problems because they have a restrictive, unforgiving religion with a wrathful god. Gorsuch, in considering the impact of Alcoholics Anonymous on alcoholism (Gorsuch, 1993) and the relationship of religion to substance abuse (Gorsuch, 1995), hypothesizes that these people can be helped to the degree that they are helped to *change* their religiousness to, for Christians, the concept of a loving God who relates to us through forgiveness.

Even such a widely accepted spirituality as Christianity has pockets of distorted faith. For example, based on my reading of the New Testament any Christianity promoting prejudice is a distorted faith. Paul's "in Christ there is neither slave nor free, Greek nor Jew, male nor female" (Galations 3:28) is a favorite of mine; it is particularly startling since he was writing to Greek slave owners in a patriarchal society. But some approaches to religion result in prejudice (Hunsberger, 1996; see Chapter 6 also) or in the self-centeredness typical of what Batson and Ventis (1993) see as the downside of spirituality.

EXERCISE

Many spirituality traditions have a principle of "you shall know them by their fruits" (Matthew 7:16). To what degree does such identification depend on social science research?

Identify an instance of what you would consider demonic spirituality.

To what degree is its identification as demonic open to data?

For the therapist or therapist to be: If something matching your definition of demonic spirituality appears in the process of treating a client, how is it appropriately treated?

For the nontherapist: When would you consider the therapist to have gone beyond the appropriate limits on this issue?

EXAMPLES OF CHRISTIAN-SPECIFIC ISSUES

The examples used in this section are ones Christian psychology students invariably discuss. They include prayer and sexuality. The former is considered separately from a discussion of spiritual resources because the concepts of prayer differ radically between, for example, Western and Eastern civilizations and between Christian and humanistic spiritualities. In like manner, the discussion of sexual ethics is from a distinctly Christian perspective that may not be held by non-Christian spiritual integrators. These two topics are included here because many readers are likely to be Christian and they may serve as illustrations for other spiritual approaches that would have their own special issues.

Prayer

Prayer comes in a variety of forms. One form is petitionary prayer. All Christians are to pray for those whom they know are in need. This means that Christian clinical psychologists will be actively praying for their clients. Such prayers are, however, between the therapist and God. They serve, as does most petitionary prayer, two purposes: First, they lift up the person in need. Second, they help the praying person focus on the needs of the other person. This type of prayer also includes prayers of the therapist for God's help for themselves, and includes a prayer immediately before seeing a client as part of the preparation for the session with the client. Prayers within a therapy session vary from unspoken personal prayers by therapist or client that the other party does not know are happening to spoken prayers.

Another form of prayer is as communion between the belief and one's higher power. As Brother Lawrence (1974) notes in his meditations, we can be dedicating by prayer to God even the cutting of loaves of bread, and so, in this sense, be praying while doing kitchen work. It would be expected that a Christian having problems or treating problems would be sufficiently in touch with God that "walking with the presence of God" prayers would be common. For a Christian, prayers outside the session and personal unspoken prayers within a session are not an issue; they are a part of all of life.

The issues of prayer in therapy center around the sharing of prayers. Is it appropriate for clinicians to tell clients that they are praying for them? Is it proper for the therapist to have an opening or concluding prayer as a standard practice? What about stopping for a moment of prayer by the therapist in the middle of the session? These issues also arise with regards to the client praying in the session.

In the absence of any research on this issue, my personal hunch is that prayer with clients may increase transference and countertransference issues (see McMinn, 1996; Sanders, 1997). A personal closeness often develops from praying together, a closeness with sufficient power that there have been occasions in the history of the church when a man and a woman were not allowed to pray together because of the closeness that would produce. This increase in transference is not always helpful in therapy.

The first issue to resolve in deciding whether to pray with a client is whether spoken prayer is used with every client. If therapists have labeled themselves as Christian, they may wish to inform all perspective clients that they start or end each session with a prayer. Providing the content of the prayer is appropriate (see later), that would seem to be an acceptable practice.

Naturally, any client who felt uncomfortable with the prayers would be encouraged to express that discomfort before any prayers were made. The therapist can then avoid prayer until the client requests it or can refer the client to another clinician. The following discussion assumes this point.

Spontaneous prayer within a session has greater problems than either an opening or closing prayer announced as a standard part of one's practice. It must feel natural to the client as well as the therapist. This is unlike most verbal input a therapist might make because it is more difficult to get feedback about prayers. If a misunderstanding occurs, spontaneous prayers may also be more difficult to reconceptualize than most other verbal input.

Even as the timing of the prayer must be natural to both client and therapist, so must the content. In particular, it must be content that strengthens the client. This may range from simple generic prayers for the client's improvement to prayers for the resolution of a specific problem to prayers for spiritual growth. Whatever the prayer, it must be consistent with encouraging religious coping styles that are known to be helpful. Hence, a prayer oriented toward cooperation with God or toward searching for and surrendering to God's will would be most appropriate. However, note that prayers that seem to encourage deferring to God can also be helpful in special cases. In particular, if the client is so bound with anxiety that they are overmotivated, they may find prayer offers temporary relief by encouraging them to trust in God's love and constant support. The anxiety drops to the level where it is an impetus to solving the cause of the anxiety. This is, as noted, a special case.

When and how to pray will vary depending on the religious background of the client. In some religious traditions prayers tend to be formal and address God with a sense of awe: "Oh Lord, we humble ourselves before you." In traditions using the "just" form of prayer—"We just want to ask you, Jesus"—the prayers are more personal and informal. Generally, the prayers of the former are less likely to ask for miracles or healing than the prayers of the latter.

It is essential for the clinician to be sensitive to the different styles of prayer and what the prayer may mean to the individual. Hopefully, the clinician already has a sense of the person's spirituality from the intake interview. The clinician should then pray in the client's style. This means that the Christian clinician generally should be able to pray in either style. While it is tempting for the clinician to feel that his or her personal and subcultural patterns of prayer are more useful, that is only a personal opinion. For clients from another religious subculture, it could be seen as a lack of understanding or a "putdown," and will generally make them feel uncomfortable. This is no help to therapy.

Prayer content covers the usual types, such as thanksgiving, confession, and intercession for the client, therapist, or others. Each of these can be appropriate if used at the proper time. But how do we define "appropriate"? Is it defined as "useful" because it may help the client adopt better coping mechanisms? Is it truly a spiritual response to the situation? Need it be one or the other?

An outline of types of classic prayers and when to use which is inappropriate here, for that is a topic that has already been richly developed in religious traditions. It is not the place of a book such as this to teach spirituality itself. Instead, the point is that the therapist must already be experienced in prayer for it to be used in therapy.

Two types of prayer are discussed in the integration literature. Tan (1997) summarizes these and provides more detail on the second type. The first is prayer used only if spiritual development is a part of the treatment. I assume that the point is that prayer must flow from the therapist's active prayer life. To interpret these discussions as saying that clinical treatment can avoid a spiritual dimension would deny the full humanness that clinical interventions require. A spiritual dimension is always involved, and if either the therapist or client actively "walks with the Lord," then a Christian spiritual element is essential in the therapy. I would certainly agree with Finney and Malony (1985a, 1985b, 1985c) that contemplative prayer is excellent, but I would not interpret these discussions to deny petitionary prayer. Certainly, the New Testament teaches that we are to call on the Lord in times of need, and therapy would be no exception.

The second type of prayer summarized by Tan (1997) is called "inner healing prayer." The focus of these prayers is on the client's internalized pain and suffering from past events that remain unresolved.

The type of past events needing such prayer are those that keep intruding into the person's thoughts and life. The procedure has been sufficiently developed so that Tan identifies seven steps in such prayers, and Seamands (1985) and Propst (1988) have written on the topic at length. It sounds appropriate, but workshop training in the method may be necessary for the Christian therapist to be able to effectively use it (if you are interested, start with Tan, 1997, and then move on to the other references).

Given the opening discussion of the difference between the psychologist's emphasis on self and at least Christian spirituality's emphasis on others, it is not surprising that intercessory prayer seems to be primarily addressed in the literature as intercessory for the client and not for others. Mowrer (1961) and Rosenhan and London (1975) are among those who find that those in need of a clinical psychologist's help have generally not only hurt themselves but have hurt others as well. Those people's hurt should also become, before therapy can be judged spiritually successful, a center of intercessory prayer by both client and therapist. Why both? Because Christians have an obligation to pray for all those for whom they know circumstances that enable us to direct prayer at a problem. Such details will become known in therapy to the therapist (the client may or may not know of these prayers by the therapist). The therapist may then be able, starting from their own prayer life, to help the client reach the point of being a servant to those whom the client has injured.

Sexuality

The Judeo traditions and the religions flowing from it—Christian and Moslem—have been unique in their approach to sex. The other religions of the Greco–Roman world were open to many forms of sex and even used sex in fertility rites and raised money by prostitution. But that was not the case for the Jews and those building upon that tradition.

Today Christians continue to hold separate standards from many others regarding sex. Sex within marriage is fine, but premarital or extramarital sex is discouraged. This is found in the research. For example, Gorsuch and Smith (1972) found a separate factor for sexual morality that was independent of a factor for general morality. Other studies (reviewed in Gorsuch, 1988; Hood et al., 1996) find that Christians are less engaged in nonmarital sex than non-Christians in the United States, with the Christian rates being half that of the non-Christians (assuming no restriction in range). (Interestingly, the sexual rate within marriage is the same for Christians as non-Christians, so repression is not the issue.) Obviously, the Christian norms are not followed by all Christians. However, social psychological research seldom finds an effect that cuts a rate in half, and so this is quite striking.

Since Christians and non-Christians have different views of sex (Gorsuch, 1988), Christian psychologists and non-Christian psychologists will have different sex values than some of their clients. Christian psychologists will have more restrictive norms than their non-Christian clients will, and non-Christian psychologists will have more lenient norms than their Christian clients will. What then is to be done if sex is a problem for the client? That question can only be answered from an integrative perspective involving clinical psychology and spirituality.

A particularly volatile sexual issue in the current cultural environment is that of homosexuality. The American Psychological Association (APA) and secular psychologists in general feel homosexuality per se is not a problem, and that the appropriate problems arising from this sexual orientation are matters of how to adapt society to the rights of homosexuals.

Christians are divided on the issue of homosexuality, but most denominations hold homosexual behavior to be unacceptable. Fulton, Gorsuch, and Maynard (1999) have shown that a primary correlate for the rejection of homosexual behavior is the belief that the Bible contains the exact words of God. In several lists of sins in the Bible, homosexual behavior is included. Those who hold most closely to the words of the Bible being the exact words of God are most likely to judge homosexuality as wrong. They feel they have no choice in this decision, since God has spoken in revelation. (In this study, there is only a little evidence of "homophobia" among Christians; while Christians who hold most closely to the words of the Bible being the words of God reject homosexuals, they reject liars and racists even more.) For such Christians the question is how a homosexual might become heterosexual or how a homosexual might lead a celibate life. Note that this is not a violation of APA ethics despite APA's stance on homosexuality, for APA ethics also clearly state that we respect the values of the client.

When a non-Christian therapist treats a Christian client or a Christian therapist treats a non-Christian client and issues of sexuality develop, our professional ethics are clear. If the values of the client and therapist differ, the therapist indicates to the client the value differences and offers to refer him or her to someone who has similar values.

For those who label themselves "Christian psychologists" this is less of a problem. Most clients would expect Christian psychologists to value heterosexual behavior within marriage as the norm. If that is not the case, then the therapist position that differs from what the client would assume needs to be stated up front with the offer to refer.

EXERCISE

What resources might your spiritual tradition bring to integrating clinical psychology and spirituality? If none come to mind, phone two people well trained in your tradition and ask them for references discussing such issues.

CHAPTER 6

Integration with Social Psychology

Social psychology is a prime area for integration of the type in which two disciplines bring their resources to bear on a common problem. That is because social psychology examines attitudes and groups, both of which are prominent in everyday life. The variety of issues that social psychology can address suggests that this will be the most prominent area of integration in the long term. While a minority of the population needs help from clinical psychologists, all of those plus those not needing help are involved in social psychology. And all clinical psychologists involve social psychology, not only because the usual therapy is a social interaction, but also because it must be a focal area for clients since they live in a social world.

The first section of this chapter uses the impact of the number of members in a group to briefly illustrate that social psychology has information about effective structures that can help spiritual organizations better achieve their goals. While there is little integration with spirituality, it does show that social psychology (including industrial and organizational psychology) addresses practical questions that may arise regarding how the size of a group affects its processes. Since spirituality has often been expressed in communities, the impact of size can be an important question.

The topics chosen for this chapter continue with a topic we have already considered through discussion of ethnocentrism: groups in cooperation and in conflict with implications for reducing conflict. Using that as a base, intolerance and stereotyping (prejudice) toward others are considered.

Social psychology has a host of other topics than those addressed in this chapter. These range from the pragmatic, such as the size of groups, to the heart of integration, as addressed in some of the other sections. The emphases of integration shift with the nature of the problem. Social psychology is a prime area for further development of integration as joint problem solving, for regardless of how else we might characterize people, we are always found in groups and are influenced by our attitudes.

The breadth of social psychological integration can be seen by what has been left out, since a chapter can only hold a few samples. The samples here were selected as to be important and yet easy to communicate. Exploring an introductory social psychology textbook or other discussions of integration in social psychology (e.g., Meyers, 1986, 1999) will provide additional ideas for integration. Altruism and leadership are two such topics not addressed here.

IMPACT OF SIZE OF GROUPS

Integration can, as noted in Chapter 1, take place on many levels. In this section the concern is with information that can make groups concerned with spirituality more effective. It is a simple principle but one that has many implications: The size of the group has a major impact on the discussion and decision making that occur.

The psychological size of the group is measured in terms of how many linkages each person in the group must make. A linkage is a possible interaction with another person that must be tracked. Here are two types at the extremes. First, consider leaderless discussion groups. The group may be discussing materials they have all read on ethics. In such a leaderless discussion group, each person must track each other person. One would not know whether to speak unless that person had tracked the current speaker to see when that person finished and had also tracked all the other members of the group to see if any of them were about to speak. We already know the limiting factor on such a group: the 5 to 9 rule of the number of things we can keep actively in mind (Miller, 1956). In terms of groups, the "things" are the people with whom we need an active linkage. We can keep a maximum of 5 to 9 such linkages active at one time. Therefore, the maximum size for a leaderless discussion group should normally be six (each one person links with five other people). Placing the number at six recognizes that it is best to go with a number that include everyone in a discussion group; the smaller number works for all.

A second example is at the other extreme, a very much large group. This could be a lecturer in a philosophy class or a minister giving a sermon to a congregation. It is impossible to conduct such a group as a leaderless discussion group. The number of possible linkages for an individual would equal the number of people in that group. By definition, a large group would have more than nine other people for each member to track and so it would exceed the 5 to 9 rule upper limit. Actually, in this type of group the leader addresses the group, not the people, and the number of linkages is generally one. Each listener has one linkage with the speaker; the speaker has one linkage with the group (although that might vary throughout the speech as the speaker notices someone in particular or some subgroup within the audience).

Most groups are intermediate in size between these two extremes. Thus, a group of a dozen may have a speaker-led discussion or split the group into subgroups of four or five for small group discussions.

Other group functions follow the $N \times (N-1)$ rule for groups in which each person has a linkage to each other person. The processes shift as a function of the square of the number of people involved. For example, it has seemed to me that the difficulty in arranging a group meeting time goes up with the number of people involved who have different schedules. When a group of three becomes a group of four it becomes twice as difficult to find a meeting time, because $3 \times (3-2) = 6$ and $4 \times (4-3) = 12$, with the latter being twice the former.

What a person gets out of a group is a function of group size. In a small group, everyone interacts with everyone else (unless there is a rule to the contrary). Personal involvement is high. In a large group, everyone interacts primarily with the leader(s). Interpersonal involvement is low. Therefore, if spirituality centers on personal involvement and interpersonal interaction, small groups are to be recommended. However, if spirituality centers on following leaders, large groups are recommended.

What do these rules about the number of people in a group have to do with spirituality? First, it can be considered natural theology, in the sense of telling us basic characteristics of humans that need to be taken into account. Second, it tells us how to effectively build groups for effective spiritual development.

There is an important way in which the information on the size of groups needs to have a commentary from spirituality. What kinds of social interaction are desired? If our worldview suggests a strong leader is desired, then we shall want groups sufficiently large that they can only function with such a leader. Groups greater than six, seven, or more work better with a clear leader to which everyone relates. If our worldview suggests the maximum number of people need to be involved (a more democratic worldview without the strong leader), then groups less than seven should be used. Here is another example: If you want it to appear that minorities are major decision makers, have them make up 40 percent of large groups appointed to reach decisions.

That large group cannot dialog about each issue in-depth, so set up subcommittees of seven people, with the major subcommittees having two minority people but representing two different minorities (so each has more in common with the majority group than with the other minority) and the chair being someone already known to have the view of the majority. The results will, on the average, reflect the majority group viewpoint much more than the minority viewpoints, but, given the number of minority members, the process will seem to empower minorities. Different sizes, and other structures under which a group function, empower different people. Who is empowered and who is not is a spiritual issue.

CONFLICT AND ITS REDUCTION

Conflict can be defined broadly or narrowly. By the broad definition, conflict includes differences of opinion that are openly debated. With this definition, some conflict is good and even essential. It stimulates the processes and assures that a wide range of options is examined. Most of us would see conflict thus defined as promoting thoughtful spirituality. This is, like group size, a useful study.

Critical to my spirituality is the difference between conflicts that engender thoughtfulness and those more extreme conflicts that harm another. The harm may be physical but is generally psychological. It includes the pain of being verbally abused or the fear arising from a group ignoring that which the person sees as a critical potential disaster.

Since my spirituality views conflict harming another as qualitatively different from problems without such harm, a narrower definition of conflict is used here that emphasizes harmful results. **Conflict is whenever "personal survival becomes the issue" (Malony, 1995b), or, in a social psychological definition, whenever normal group processes break down because of disagreements among the participants.** The harm is the perceived threat to the person or the breakdown of group processes. For example, when the board of an organization discusses and votes on a resolution to resolve the same issue for the third month in a row, the normal process is no longer resolving the issues.

Spirituality has several relationships to cooperation and conflict. Most spirituality paradigms are obstensibly "all for cooperation and all against conflict." But that is not always the way it works out. In fact, spirituality's relationship to conflict ranges widely. For example, members of some spirituality subcultures are pressured by the majority culture, and the pressure may grow to open conflict. Or members of spirituality groups may serve as mediators between other groups in conflict, as has occurred surprisingly often in international politics (Johnston & Sampson, 1994).

As noted in the discussion of evil, spirituality in the form of idealism may itself produce conflict (Baumeister, 1997). In that case, spirituality supports a position that becomes an absolute ideal, sweeping all else before it. "Witch hunts" are conducted to identify those who "are against righteousness" so that they may be purged. History shows such idealism "runs wild" in wars based on religion. So spiritual movements have had close contact with the problem of conflict, ranging from being the victims of it to being the instigators of it.

Social psychology has much research that is applicable to the question of conflict. Literature quoted here ranges from game theory to research on labeling effects to realistic group conflict theory, each of which has information for dialoging with spirituality. Each is a detailed research program itself.

The goal of this section is to help spiritual movements understand how to prevent and reduce conflict, both within their own movements and with other movements. This is not to say that spirituality should always avoid conflict. Spirituality involves ethics, and ethics means that we may need to take a position that causes conflict. However, I do hold that my Christian spirituality means that we should avoid conflict unless ethics and the situation allow no other possibility, and minimize the conflict if avoidance does not work. In keeping with a long Christian tradition, mediating conflicts among others is also mentioned.

Conflict Perspectives

While spiritualities generally agree that conflict is best avoided, there is still a wide range of opinions on what is or is not acceptable conflict (Clouse, 1991). A major difference is in how violence is judged. Some hold that violence is appropriate in situations that cannot be resolved any other way. This has given rise to the idea of *jihad* and "just wars." For *jihad*, the conflict between religions may justify violence and, for "just wars," the innocent or wronged party is entitled at least to self-defense. Of course, the definition of "innocent" and "wronged" are from each group's own perspective.

"Just war" is the position that war is just if it meets certain conditions (e.g., see Brown, 1991; Holmes, 1991; Mouw, 1992, for a succinct overview). Self-defense against unprovoked aggression—with aggression including any act intended to harm another—is an example of a just war. Just war is a situation for which psychological information takes second place to ethical judgments. We know that both physical and psychological damage from the violence will be extensive, but the good that results—providing that side wins—outweighs the damage that is done. In its more perverse (at least in my ethics) forms, it may be argued that the violence is best for the recipient: "We are doing it for their own good!" Those killed in the Inquisition were seen as spiritually purified when they confessed their sins just before they were executed. "Just war" is also found in warrior societies, where the actions of the heroes are the fodder for legends and ballads extolling their courage and honor—and is currently hallowed in movies.

Exhibit 6.1 gives some historic data on a military action that almost all—at least among the Allies—have claimed to be justified: the entry of the United States into World War II. Individual physical and psychological damage was great, but "it needed to be done."

EXHIBIT 6.1
World War II: A Just War for the United States?

Most in the United States viewed entry into World War II as justified. The surprise attack of the Japanese on Hawaii and the nonstop aggression of Hitler in Europe were the bases of the justification of our involvement, for good was on the side of the Allies.

Many died, and many were injured. Among my relatives was Clyde Spittler, who flew for the Navy in the Pacific. He was declared an "ace" when he shot down his fifth enemy plane. But there was a price to be paid. On one mission his plane was damaged and his crewman died from wounds on the way back. Can you imagine what it would be like to be flying as fast as you can to safety while listening to your friend dying? The price did not end with the war, for posttraumatic stress plagued him. The family rallied around to help him throughout the rest of his life, but I never heard any complaint about his involvement in the war, for it had been necessary given the attack by the Japanese.

RBC notes that the European war was seen as justified, turning people who were normally pacifists into supporters of this war. One slogan ran, "War is hell. Hitler is worse. Stop Hitler now" (Cattell, 1972).

The problem of just war theory is in its application. As might be expected from the nature of ethnocentrism, there is precedent for "us" concluding that "our side is just." It should not be surprising to find both sides of a conflict claiming to be innocent and wronged. While criteria for a just war can be established, they are of little help in the face of ethnocentrism unless there is a recognized noninvolved party to apply those principles, a party that can enforce the decision. During the early middle ages the Pope was able to occasionally serve this function between states since the Pope was independent of any state. Excommunication was the threat that enforced the decrees (people took their Christianity so seriously that the threat of excommunication was a force in politics). However, without such an outside party, just war theory falls victim to ethnocentrism so often that it is not a psychologically viable position.

The antitheses of just war spiritualities hold that any violence is wrong. Pacifism, as compared to another approach presented later, then goes further to reject violence regardless of what the other side of the conflict does. Pacifism rejects all violence, but it is not to be confused with indifference or a lack of action. Instead, the pacifist discussed here is actively engaged in the issues, resisting aggression by nonviolent means.

Pacifism is supported by several rationales (see, e.g., Augsburger, 1994; Holmes, 1991). The first rationale discussed here focuses on the impact of one's pacifism as an effective tool and model for others; the second discussion is of the rationale that focuses on the pacifist commitment to acting righteously regardless of whether there is any impact on others.

The rationale based on the impact of one's pacifism as a model for others holds that nonviolent resistance places the aggressor in a very difficult position, that of harming innocents and those who refuse to inflict violence. To do such violence is offensive to themselves or to outsiders, who then put a stop to the aggression.

Nonviolent resistance can work. The 1950s to 1970s civil rights movement in the United States used nonviolent resistance well. The aggressors knew the danger of "making martyrs," and what the press would do if innocents or nonviolent people were harmed. I call this the "pragmatic rationale" for pacifism. Since it is pragmatic, psychology is called on to evaluate if it works.

The pragmatic rationale may propose an effect of pacifism on the aggressor regardless of outsiders: "If we model cooperation and nonviolence, they will do the same and be cooperative and nonviolent." But does cooperation change a noncooperative person to be cooperative? These types of interactions have been investigated by game theory research (see Myers, 1993; Orkin, 1999, for overviews). In game situations, a person can choose to cooperate or to "rip off" the other player. Many do "rip off" the other person if that is a profitable action.

How is the "rip-off" of the cooperative person prevented and cooperation gained? The person who may become the victim states clearly that they will cooperate, although this gives the other person the opportunity to harm them. Nevertheless, they put a stipulation on it: "If you do rip me off, I will retaliate the first chance I get." And they do retaliate the first time they can after the other person takes advantage of them. Then they put another stipulation: "I shall cooperate again, but remember what I do if you do not respond cooperatively." Then the opponent plays cooperatively. If no retaliation is taken after the first violation, the aggression continues unabated. While it is true such social psychological research does not involve the extremes of real life—physical violence is not involved—this research suggests that **cooperative strategies work only if there is force backing them up** to control the person with no morals against violence (Axelrod, 1980; Orkin, 1999). Granted that this is not the ideal world toward which many spiritualities strive. In that world that we seek to bring into existence, pacificism would always work.

Nonviolent resistance for civil rights worked, but the question is what made it work. Given the research just noted, it may have worked because there were occasionally riots that made the community leaders willing to work with the nonviolent people rather than risk riots. Or it may have worked because outsiders threatened economic sanctions ("We won't be able to do business with you again; too many of our buyers are upset with how you treated the protesters"). In general, it seems that the critical elements for the success of nonviolent resistance in the world of 2000 include either an aggressor with a code of honor or a public that is the "swing vote" and knows what is happening. In the civil rights movements, local citizens saw what was happening and negotiated to keep the problems from increasing.

In cases where neither of these elements—honor among the aggressors nor publicity—are present, nonviolence produces no change. Consider Stalin, who murdered literally millions of his own people and stayed in power because of it. Fasting Irish in 1920 died of starvation in prison, but that had no impact on the continuing conflict in Ireland (Augsburger, 1992, p. 79). Consider the American native peoples for whom nonviolence produced the same result as violence. (The movies *The Milagro Beanfield War* [1988] and *Thunderheart* [1992], based on actual events, illustrate how nonviolence sometimes needs force to make it effective). Pacifism can be an excellent pragmatic in the right conditions.

Some would say that pacifism based on the pragmatic rationale that it works is not true pacifism. "True" pacifism adds the "righteousness rationale." It is based on one's being righteous and has several elements to it. It begins with the assumption that it does not matter that pacifism has no effect on the other, and that the pacifist may well be injured or killed. (If this assumption is not granted, then the only rationale is the one just discussed, because it is pragmatic in the end.) To this is added the "two wrongs don't make a right" rationale. We should be righteous ourselves—nonviolent—regardless of what the other person does and regardless of whether our actions have any impact on another. We should never, in a conflict, lower ourselves to the level of an opponent so unrighteous as to use violence. This is a reasonably straightforward rationale if the conflict involves only the pacifist and the other person.

It is a rare conflict that involves only two people. Even in the situation of a robber and victim alone on a street, others are implicitly involved. For example, the family of the pacifist will be impacted if the pacifist is hurt or killed. Of course, if groups are involved the decisions made will directly affect many others. Surrendering or failing to add to a war effort may indeed affect others. A pacifist's position that he or she is the only one that may be harmed because of the pacifism is seldom tenable.

Since the pacifist position puts others in harm's way, an additional element is required to justify nonpragmatic pacifism: a definition of responsibility that places it all on the aggressor. If the pacifist avoids violence that may be necessary to stop an aggressor from hurting another, and if that other person is hurt, it is the responsibility of the aggressor and not of the pacifist. The aggressor was the sanctioning agent and not the pacifist. Hence, the pacifist maintains righteous perfection even if others are harmed.

The pacifist definition of responsibility is somewhat unique. It defines sin in this case as only the "sin of commission" (a result arising from one's own action), and not the "sin of omission" (a result arising from failing to act). It is akin to Pilate's washing his hands of the Jesus problem: Allow the mob to decide that the Romans should kill him (Matthew 27:24). Pacifists are aware of the problem and stand ready to do everything they can short of violence to stop the aggression, even giving up their own lives. But their commitment to using other means is a key issue only for the pragmatic rationale for pacifism. The righteousness rationale must hold even when nonviolent intervention is a total failure. In that case, the innocent still suffer, and the responsibility must be laid at the feet of the aggressor and not the pacifist for the pacifist to still be righteous.

Some psychological research (e.g., locus of control) and ethicists, and the current author, would define responsibility as arising from the ability or power to change the outcome. If we could change the outcome and do not, then we are also responsible for the outcome. These are sins of omission (this does not reduce the responsibility of the aggressors, since they too had the power to change the outcome). Jesus uses this logic of responsibility when he notes that people will be judged because they failed to help the hungry, the stranger, or the person in jail (Matthew 25:41–46). From this view of responsibility, the pacifist's knowingly avoiding violence that has a reasonable chance of saving others is then sacrificing others to preserve their personal righteousness. But by doing so, righteous is not preserved, for they have committed a sin of omission against the innocent injured party.

Denying responsibility by a failure to act may be appropriate in some spiritual paradigms but it is hard to justify with a paradigm that says "greater love has no one than this, that a person lay down his or her life for his or her friends" (John 15:13) and stresses being the servant of others. This rationale places obligations toward others above oneself, while pacifism places one's own righteousness above obligation to others.

In conversations with pacifists, there is sometimes another rationale. It comes down to the statement, "But there are always other ways." I wish it were so, and strongly support social psychological research and the development of spirituality to help this become true! In the meantime, it must rest upon the pacifist to prove that there is another way. I suspect it is a position easier to hold about someone else's conflicts than if you are a leader caught in the midst of a conflict—and particularly difficult if you are the victim.

EXERCISE

Watch the 1993 movie *Schindler's List*. Note in particular the nonviolent resisters, such as the family that refused to separate. Considering the nature of the Nazi government, is there any nonviolent action that could have been taken by the first Jews and Poles arrested that would have had a reasonable chance of preventing the holocaust?

My position is between just war and pacifism, and can be called the "lesser-of-the-evils" position. The lesser-of-the-evils position agrees with the just war theory that it may be necessary to do violence, but, in agreement with pacifism, does not "heroize" it but holds it only as the last, terrible option. Instead of implying that any war is "good," it states that violence is never good. Nor is war something that purifies and validates warriors. People can arise to meet the challenge in spite of personal sacrifice, as in Exhibit 6.1, and show commendable loyalty and courage. Nevertheless, the results of war are still horrible, and it is hard to see enough good occurring to offset the hell of war.

Not responding to aggression may result in an even worse situation. Exhibit 6.1 was introduced because that war illustrates this line of thinking. Hitler intended to conquer everything in sight and practiced genocide. What would have happened if the United States had taken a pacifism stance? If Hitler would have been allowed just a little more time, his scientists likely would have produced powerful new weapons. Given Hitler's ambitions and his past behavior, do we care to speculate what the world would be like if we had stayed out of that war? War is hell, but sometimes the alternative is an even worse hell.

When violence is seen as bad and only as a last resort, then the emphasis is on seeking other options whenever possible. The lesser-of-the-evils position joins the pacifists in urging social scientists to work on better options so that it is not one evil versus another but rather a choice, including peaceful resolution of major conflicts. Anyone serious about preventing violence is urged to study more about how this is done (Johnston & Sampson, 1994, give numerous examples from international situations). Violence should only be considered when "just peace" (Stassen, 1992) and mediation efforts using principles such as those discussed here have been tried. In fact, we should be optimistic about the chances of avoiding violence. Some document that Christian mediation has often worked "behind the scenes" to reduce violence. Indeed, I consider Stassen to be essential reading for those concerned with these issues.

Whenever the first rationale for pacifism—that it is an effective tool—does work, the lesser-of-the-evils approach supports pacifism; this is classically referred to as nonviolent resistance. It was the centerpiece of the successful civil rights movement. The position, however, disagrees with pacifism's position that a person's own righteousness is more important than what happens to others. Instead, it holds that others are very important, and even more important than oneself. A person may choose to "bloody myself" so that "someone else goes unbloodied." Nevertheless, given the discussion of ethnocentrism in judging a just war, we must hesitate to move to violence because it could be more our rationalization than a proper decision. Indeed, as long as there is any possibilities of using nonviolent resistance that might work, it is the first line of action.

Discussions of pacificism generally define violence in terms of war and other acts of physical violence. Psychology has a major critique of those discussions: Emotional violence is just as important as physical violence and should be judged the same.

EXERCISE

1. Rank order the following events as to how upsetting they would be for someone unprepared for such an event.

   • Being fired for unethical behavior that you did not do.

   • Losing your parents' retirement investments because your business partner lied to you.

   • A loved one abandoning you to your fate because it would be too inconvenient for them to help you.

   • Being stopped by police who obviously want to arrest you for something you did not do.

   • Having a friend never speak to you again without explaining why.

   • Being in the midst of a "church fight" in which your former friends shout at you—and vice versa—so that you can neither eat nor sleep.

- Losing your child's love, and probably never seeing them again, from their peers' influence.

- Being thrown into jail in a foreign country and not being allowed to contact anyone.

- Learning after a month of having the ideal romantic relationship that your date only did it to win a bet.

2. List two other events that you would nominate as being more upsetting than most on this list.

While physical violence leaves emotional scars, many other interactions leave as bad or even worse emotional scars. I have helped churches handle difficult conflict problems and have often found severe spiritual damage with posttraumatic stress responses such as anxiety, stopping eating, and flashbacks. Some of the hurt people will never enter a church again. This type of violence also needs to be examined so that we may reduce all modes of violence. When we reduce the modeling of physical violence in the movies and TV programs (Smith & Donnerstein, 1998), hopefully we can also reduce the modeling of emotional violence as well. When it is all said and done, it may well be that "soap operas" have encouraged more psychological damage to people than any other type of movie or TV show, including those featuring physical violence.

The lesser-of-the-evils approach must, to truly be the "lesser," minimize damage of all kinds to everyone. There is no vengence, no unwarranted harm, whether physical or mental. Mouw (1992) stresses this point by noting that even when we must do regrettable actions, they still should be done with civility (and even kindness whenever possible).

Given the present definition of conflict, all conflict hurts people and leaves scars. Moreover, with the definition of violence including emotional as well as physical, all conflict is engaging in violence against others. If we ever choose to engage in either type of violence, we must have a case so strong that no one may argue that it is the result of our ethnocentric bias.

Summary of Lesser-of-the-Evils Approach

1. Harm includes not just physical but emotional harm.

2. Sins of omission are just as wrong as sins of commission. Hence, allowing harm to an innocent party when we could have prevented it is wrong (an evil "act" if it is done deliberately). The fact that someone else commits a sin of commission does not relieve us of our guilt if we allow that sin by a failure to stop it; it just means there are two guilty parties, one from a sin of com-

mission and one from a sin of omission. Hence, the person who could have but did not save another's life is guilty for the loss of that life. In speaking of helping the hungry, thirsty, and jailed, Jesus said, "As you did not do it to one of the least of these, you did it not to me" (Matthew 25:45).

3. Deliberate harm of another is always wrong. Thus, harming a person's business by boycotting, for example, is wrong since it does damage to the owner, the employees, and probably the customers. Or communicating in anger that leaves a permanent scar or drives someone out of an organization is wrong (in some cases, it would be more evil than taking a life if you hold that salvation is more important than life). Harm, whether caused by omission or commission, is to be avoided even if it is personally expensive to do so.

4. An act or non-act that causes harm should be done only to prevent an even greater harm. Thus, I publicly encouraged boycotting of specific restaurants refusing to serve people of color because the business's prejudicial practices caused, in my estimation, even greater harm. But harm was done to the owner and employees. My good intent does not remove that harm (or make it good). In my view, harming a criminal is a lesser evil than allowing the criminal to harm an innocent party (although I recommend always seeking an alternative that would do no harm to either).

5. All decisions that may involve harm to another need to be considered in light of our propensity to make errors. For example, taking the life of another is so permanent we must be very careful in such decisions. And doing a "mean" act so that "the other person can learn better" is doubtful, particularly when we benefit from it (e.g., we enjoy doing it).

6. Many human situations are such that we only get to choose the lesser of the evils we do. We must depend on God's grace for forgiveness for the sins of omission and commission that we do in such situations.

7. The better way to avoid being forced into a sinful, violent act is to work hard at preventing the situation from reaching that point.

I disagree with the pacifist only in rare extreme situations. The classical example is when killing a criminal is the only way to prevent the criminal killing an innocent party. But ethics must provide direction even for those extreme cases (and help us develop ways to avoid those extremes).

Causes of Conflict

My understanding of the sources of conflict uses what I call a "two-factor theory of conflict." The two factors leading to conflict are labeling and competitive goals. The former, labeling, refers to the using of group names. The later, competitive goals, are those that (1) can be achieved by one group but (2) prevent another group from achieving that group's goal. Either alone can be the basis for conflict, but both together are more likely to produce conflict.

For an example of the problems of labeling, consider a church that has an earlier and a later morning worship service. It is common for the earlier service to be more informal than the later service. That service may draw those who like praise songs more than hymns. As time passes, the people attending the early service get to know each other better than they do the people attending the later service, and vice versa. The later service becomes known to attract those who like hymns more than songs, and they get to know each other better than they get to know those attending the early service.

We then have people who begin to identify with the label "early service" or "late service." The natural course of events leading to conflicts is for these labels to begin to be used widely; then people identify even more strongly with their group and ethnocentrism is engaged: "We are better than they." Ethnocentrism results from labeling rather than being a cause of labeling, but some wishing to promote ethnocentrism will encourage labeling to produce the ethnocentrism that produces the labeling. Or perhaps it is better to consider them "two sides of the same coin."

Ethnocentrism includes stereotyping, so a person is judged primarily by the service they attend. "J. is an 'early service' person. The early service consists of those who want unstructured services, so J. won't want to serve on the worship committee which lays out the worship structure for the year." Of course, only some who attend the early service do so because it is more informal. Others attend because they must work later that day, because they are naturally early risers, because a member of their family often leads the early service, and so forth. Deciding about J. based solely on the service attended, called stereotyping, does J. a major injustice. When J. hears it, the labeling is stepped up: "Did you hear what those late church people did? They kept J. off the worship committee just because J. goes to the early service. And J. would have loved being on it."

Labeling can lay a foundation for conflict. Exhibit 6.2 illustrates a conflict that began with labeling.

Exhibit 6.2
The Color Barrier: A.D. 527

Constantinople, A.D. 527. Justinian had just become Emperor. Having been raised in the palace, he was ready. His first edict was to "support the innocent and to chastise the guilty of every denomination and color" (Gibbon, 1776/1990, pp. 652–655). Here are some of the problems caused by color discrimination:

- Preferences were given in jobs.
- Judges shaded their decisions based on color.
- Creditors of one color were forced to give up any attempt at collecting what they were owed by someone of another color.
- A governor hanged two assassins who had killed his servant in an attempt to kill him. However, the assassins were of the "right" color and he of the "wrong" color. So the empress had the governor hanged.
- One group invited the other to the Hippodrome for a meeting but failed to tell their guests that swords were allowed. The guests were slaughtered.
- The conflict based on color raged for at least 300 years.

"Color" means color of skin today, but the colors in Constantinople were the "blues" versus the "greens." From what Gibbon reports, the starting point of the blues and greens was chariot races. The rigs were colored blue or green so that the chariots could be identified at a distance. As far as I could tell, these were not even teams, but they were labels. People became known as those who supported the "blue" or the "green" racers. And what probably started as fun "kidding around" became labels applied to people. With the labels in place, conflict built around them.

Commentary: How important could this trivial labeling become? Gibbon estimates that 30,000 people were killed in the blue–green conflict. Our own experience with another labeling seen as having no intrinsic value by psychologists and Christians—race—also tells us that trivial labeling can be dangerous.

The second factor of my two-factor theory of conflict is based on competitive goals. **With competitive goals, the achievement of one group's goals prevents the other group from achieving their goals.** Exhibit 6.3 illustrates the process.

Exhibit 6.3
Boys Camp: A Straight Course from Competition to Conflict

Sherif, Harvey, White, Hood, and Sherif (1961) and Sherif and Sherif (1969) ran several boys camps to examine how groups formed and how leadership developed. They took groups of boys to Robber's Cave State Park. The boys were housed in several cabins.

The first day, the boys started playing games, such as baseball. There were other contests also, all competitions between the cabins. Each cabin formed its own teams and chose names for them: Labeling had appeared.

The second day, the groups selected leaders and plotted strategies. There were more competitive games. They only sat with "guys like us" at dinner; that is, boys from their own cabin. Ethnocentrism had appeared.

The third day, the boys got serious. They knew they were better than the other groups, so the only reason they lost must have been because the other cabin cheated. Ethnocentrism was in full force.

Boys threw food at boys from other cabins. One group marked up another cabin by writing insulting statements. That cabin began planning to retaliate, in full force. Conflict had appeared.

The psychologists found that competition produced a common enemy for all the boys in one cabin: the other cabins. A common enemy produced strong groups, and the groups were hostile. Very hostile.

It developed fast—very fast. It was only Wednesday evening—the boys would be there the rest of the week.

Competition involves and reinforces groups. Groups are always ethnocentric, overvaluing themselves and undervaluing others. This lays the groundwork for conflict. Competition both produces ethnocentric groups and gives them reasons to enter into conflict against each other.

Prevention and Reduction of Conflict

Historically we have seldom been very successful in preventing or reducing conflict. Justinian certainly was not, and the blue–green conflict continued for years. Hopefully our scientific knowledge of conflict enables us to do better. My personal experience in mediating conflicts suggests that we have powerful principles that can indeed help us to do better, principles that involve the integration of psychology and spirituality.

The prevention and reduction of conflict follow directly from its causes: labeling and the types of goals. In the former it is a matter of preventing labeling from occurring or reducing its impact when it is necessary to have labels. For the latter it is the elimination of competitive goals to prevent conflict and the establishment of interdependent goals for eliminating the possibility of conflict and for reducing labeling.

The following discussion uses examples to illustrate. However, this is not a training guide to conflict prevention or reduction. That would require a separate book and appropriate experience. The point is to illustrate how integrating spirituality with social psychology can be helpful.

Labeling, the first basis for conflict in the two-factor theory of conflict, is reduced by first realizing the dangers so we can become self-conscious of using labels. Then we can purposefully reduce them. For example, consider the church with an early and late worship service. The former is shorter and less formal, while the latter is both longer and more formal. This is fine, unless people become identified with the service they attend. Then the issue is "Will the early service support this?" or "What will be the reaction of the late service people?"

EXERCISE

Listen to the conversation of others. Watch for labels in use, such as "we" versus "they." Then watch your own conversation for labels. Do you really need them? What else could be used instead of the we–they labels?

What do we do instead of using labels? We shift to individual difference language. Instead of saying "the early service people," we say "those who have to work Sunday afternoons" or "those who prefer more informal services" or "those who like to get up earlier," and so forth. Note that we are being more accurate also, for we speak to the property that is really at issue. By speaking to that, we are more accurate as well as avoiding labeling. Which of these three phrases we use would vary depending on what the issue truly was.

We also reduce the relevance of labels by interweaving the members of the early and late services whenever possible. For all other groups the early and late service people are interwoven together. The same group is never formed twice, but the members of all groups are varied; early service people never form all of a committee, but each committee has some. In the prevention mode, interweaving would be achieved by quiet monitoring by the leaders. This is done without fanfare, for to request each service to have "representatives" on each committee would emphasize the groups, reinforcing and even requiring labeling.

For example, in a church conflict mediation one question was whether the church was gaining or losing more members because of the new minister. I had a committee appointed that consisted of the most prominent leaders of the two groups that had formed around this issue. (That scared some people, who thought there would be "blood on the walls if you get them together." The committee worked out only because of the type of goal they were given, as noted later.) When the committee reported to the congregation, the church members saw them sitting together, talking together, and defending each other's parts of the joint report. For some members this was a serious blow to the labeling that had occurred. The boundaries between the two groups were blurred. (Also, whenever a label was used I asked what the speaker meant in individual difference terms rather than in labels, and always pointed out the wide range of positions actually in the "group." "Do you mean those in class X who joined after the minister came here or those who joined before?")

Superordinate Goals

In addition to the first factor of conflict, labeling, we can also use the second factor of conflict, superordinate (also known as interdependent) goals, to prevent or reduce conflict. It has already been noted that competitive goals breed conflict. Another type of goal, interdependent, reduces conflict.

Neutral goals occur when one group's achieving of its goals neither helps nor hinders the other group achieving its goals. Neutral and cooperative goals, at best, only postpone conflict rather than reduce it. With neutral goals, the groups "just do their own thing," and the other groups are irrelevant. But it does not change any of their concepts or attitudes toward the other groups. When they come back together, the attitudes toward each other are found to have been just "put on hold."

Cooperative goals are those where groups help each other achieve goals. To reach cooperative goals, both groups work together until the goal is reached. They may, for example, appoint representatives to joint task forces. While an occasional friendship is developed that lowers tensions between the groups, nothing has really changed with regard to the group relationships before the cooperation was initiated. Once the need for the cooperation is past, the group relationship is redefined in terms of the next set of goals. They still remain separate groups (with the resulting labeling and ethnocentrism).

The impact of cooperation is clearly seen among countries or segments of a political party with a common enemy. They cooperate until the common enemy (e.g., another's candidate for president) is defeated, but then scrap among themselves. Cooperative goals slow conflict or postpone it until the cooperative goal is reached, but only occasionally reduce conflict.

Cooperative goals will produce contact, and it is a common misperception that contact is all that is needed. Social psychology has conclusively proved that it is the type of contact that is important (Sherif et al., 1961). Some types of contact reduce ethnocentrism but others produce it. That is determined by the goals under which contact occurs. For example, contact in the midst of competitive goals increases conflict.

The type of goal most helpful to preventing and reducing conflict is what Sherif and colleagues (1961) and Sherif and Sherif (1969) called superordinate or interdependent goals. **Superordinate goals require**

the work of both groups for anyone to reach his or her goal. Note this difference from cooperative goals, for it is extremely important: The others are *required* to reach one's own goals (which is the definition of interdependent or superordinate goals). With a cooperative goal, the goal may be achieved without the aid of the other group if one's group simply works harder or finds a third group with which to cooperate. The other group is not indispensable. An interdependent goal exists only when the other group is indispensable. Exhibit 5.4 illustrates Sherif and colleagues' use of superordinate goals.

EXHIBIT 6.4
The Boy's Camp Survives

In Exhibit 6.3, we left the boys in serious conflict.

That Wednesday night the psychologists running the camp met together and decided to try a superordinate goal to reduce the conflicts. At the end of the meeting one went out to the water truck and moved it to just before a ridge at the top of a road down a hill. When leaving the truck, the headlights were switched on.

The next day the truck was needed to go after water. Because the headlights had been on all night, the battery was dead, and so the truck would not start. The boys gathered around and decided that if the truck were at the top of the ridge, it could be started by rolling it down the slope on the other side of the ridge.

One cabin tried to move the truck by pushing it. It was too heavy for them to move alone.

Another cabin tied a rope to it. They were not strong enough to pull it alone.

After much debate among the boys, they finally all pushed and pulled. The truck moved. It rolled down the hill and started.

The rest of the week the activities involved one superordinate goal after another. Nothing was done by cabin.

By the end of the week the boys no longer labeled themselves or the other cabins. Labeling had died. On the bus home, the boys of each cabin mixed and sat together. Ethnocentrism had died. They were all friendly with each other. Conflict had died.

Superordinate goals generally involve veto power of any subgroup over the combined group's actions. This requires each to really dialogue with the other. It requires a common paradigm being developed between the groups and breaks down the barriers. Indeed, if it continues long enough and there are no side conditions that forbid it, the groups merge into one group. There are no longer groups to which to return when they have reached the superordinate goal.

While social psychology has established the principle that superordinate goals prevent and heal conflict, it has no way of determining what superordinate goals are worthwhile. True, psychology can provide evidence that may make the decision much easier, but without spirituality psychology can only use common cultural values. Any detailed evaluation comes from spirituality.

The superordinate goal can be long term and vague, such as "showing the love of God to our world by how we treat each other," but it will only relate when it is made relevant to that immediate interaction. Indeed, when working with a group in conflict I generally start meetings with a short meditation (very short; people in conflict want to start overpowering the other side, not listen to someone speaking platitudes). The meditation reminds them of their spirituality's superordinate goals, but it needs to come down to the immediate interaction to help them change. So with a Christian group I use the "love chapter" (I Corinthians 13) and stress that a "goal for tonight's meeting" is for each to help their friends act out that chapter in the meeting itself. I tell them the meeting will be unsuccessful unless all help each other explore the conflict differences as Christians in that meeting.

In the example used here that brought leaders of conflicting groups into one committee, the process worked only because a clear superordinate goal was established and enforced that was consistent with the group's spirituality. (I sat in as an observer for the first meeting to get them started right, was available by phone for the next, and then they worked fine on their own.) That goal was that no one could be placed on the list of having joined before or after the minister came unless everyone on the committee agreed.

The superordinate goal for a group in conflict varies depending on the nature of the conflict and the nature of their common spirituality. Often one area of contention is "who did what when" because of the rumors that develop. Then the superordinate goal for the group is to identity the facts of what happened. "Facts" are defined as events that all observers can agree to, so everyone on this committee had to agree to a fact before it could be in the report. Facts include such things as "J. and B. talked that evening. J. reported leaving thinking they had agreed to meet the next week but B. reported thinking they would talk later about meeting the next week."

In the example of a committee with a superordinate goal, the group worked together and gave their report. It was a first step, and so only reduced the conflict, but it enabled us to move to another step.

Sometimes superordinate goals are opposed because people wish to keep their separate traditions, although they still wish to reduce and avoid conflict. "Keeping traditions" may be part of the process by defining the superordinate goal so as to include both traditions. In a church attempting to reconcile peoples of liberal and conservative theological positions, the goal needs to be having those two groups in communion. "We can not be the church we are called to be without both liberals and conservatives. So we welcome and cherish you, liberal and conservative." The goal of communion cannot be achieved if either breaks off, so both are essential. Still, some separate identity is maintained, for how else would they know if they had both? This means, of course, that the labeling will provide a good seedbed for conflict to grow; it warrants constant monitoring.

Superordinate goals have an additional advantage. Because they are powerful in drawing people together, they break down group barriers. The more comprehensive the superordinate goals, the more the barriers break down and the groups disappear. As the barriers come down, so do all the effects of labeling and ethnocentrism. No longer is a person judged as "not very smart, since they are a part of those Xs," but each person is judged by his or her potential contribution to the superordinate goal. Note the result of the superordinate goals in Exhibit 6.4. Not only did it create an atmosphere of cooperation, but boys from different cabins sat together on the way home.

If superordinate goals do bring down labeling and its effects, why be concerned with labeling as well as superordinate goals? Because it is faster to break up the labeling while also developing superordinate goals. As the group labels drop out of use, it is easier for each person to be seen as an individual helping achieve the goal, rather than as "the person group X sent us."

Competition with other groups is often used to provide a superordinate goal for that group. This is called "the common enemy approach" and can be seen in use by politicians. They identify an enemy (e.g., fascism or communism) in the hope this will bring together otherwise disparate factions. "Only if we all get behind X will we be able to stop them." The "them" may be any other group, including the other political candidate most likely to win the election. It does provide a clear and often compelling superordinate goal.

The problem with using competition with another group as an intragroup superordinate goal is that it also creates a competitive goal with that other group. This creates conflict with the other group. They, of course, will also be strengthed by this action, for the other group has a superordinate goal forced upon them, the competition. That conflict, once started, can grow with the consequence of a conflict on a larger scale between the two groups that are now competitive. The dangers are very real, and so competition with other groups to give our group a superordinate goal is seldom recommended unless it is closely controlled and special techniques are used to prevent the conflict. Exhibit 6.5 contains an example of using competition but avoiding labeling so that the competition does not itself breed conflict.

EXHIBIT 6.5
The Fun of Competition, the Impossibility of Conflict

Competition is a powerful technique for getting people to work together, and it can be fun. Bronfenbrenner (1970) reports that some countries, such as Russia and Switzerland, use it in classrooms. Instead of individuals competing to find the right answer, groups compete to learn a task. The within-group goal is to help each other learn the material until everyone in the group is able to do the task. The first group to achieve this goal wins. The competition adds fun and excitement and uses an effective teaching technique: peer instruction. It also teaches that cooperation with others does work and teaches students how to work effectively in groups, as well as teaching the academic material.

But how do they avoid the problems of competitive groups? Normally each person starts being labeled as a member of Group X or Group Y, and ethnocentrism grows from that. They avoid the problems by varying the group memberships from one contest to another. No two contests ever contain exactly the same children. Here are some procedures for dividing a classroom into groups:

- Each row of the children's desks in the classroom is the basis for a team.
- Each column of desks is a team.
- Those with birthdays ending with two are a team; those ending with three are another team, etc.
- Count off by fives (going across rows)
- Count off by fives (going down columns)

Commentary: Since there are no consistent groups, labeling and ethnocentrism never stand a chance of developing. This is an excellent example of interweaving people across groups.

Exhibit 6.5 illustrates both interweaving and superordinate goals. The former is seen in the way children are assigned to groups, the latter by the fact that the group finishes its task only when all children have mastered the lesson. As long as one remains untaught, the group keeps working (perhaps the fact that some American children would see this as unfair shows the inexperience of our children with working in true groups).

One wonders about the wide use of team competition with children in our society. Many nonschool activities—from chess clubs to soccer teams—are based on competition. It does train people how to cooperate in a group, but might it not also train in an "either they or we" mentality? Is that way of thinking helpful in international politics? Is that way of thinking one reason the United States is a legally oriented society, with so many disputes turned into a win–lose competition for a court's decision?

Exhibit 6.6 is the Beyondist position to prevent conflict between groups. It is built on the evolutionary principle that some groups will be evolutionary survivors and some not.

EXHIBIT 6.6
The Beyondist View of Cultural Conflict

RBC (Cattell, 1987) bases Beyondism in evolutionary ethics. Evolution is based on the survival of the best adapted, so groups and cultures survive based on adapting better than other groups. RBC recognizes that this could be a harsh dictum, leading to "cutthroat" competition with no quarter given.

RBC does not, however, recommend the competitive approach. Instead, we should use one of those characteristics that best distinguish us from other species: our intelligence. We should put our intelligence to use by establishing research institutions that aid us in predicting when a group is not likely to survive.

RBC himself published a number of articles identifying characteristics of nations using quantitative data and statistical analyses. He also used the same techniques to trace changes in the characteristics of countries across time. This provides evidence that the type of research he suggests is doable.

All cultural groups would be provided the information developed by the research centers. The information would be detailed enough to help groups make their own choices. Perhaps they would be content to being an evolutionary "dead end," or perhaps they would prefer to change in some manner consistent with their own values that would give them a better chance to thrive.

The Beyondist proposal to cooperate with evolution also reduces the possibilities of conflict. A nation would not have to wage war against another if it knew the other would wither away as an evolutionary "dead end." More important, it would prevent thoughtful nations committed to Beyondism from reaching the point where war was the last viable option.

An interesting outcome that RBC identifies is that people in a Beyondist world would not be eliminated from the genetic pool (or from life!) if a culture ended. Instead, they (or their children) would change cultures. This was a common occurrence, for example, in the Native American cultures of Oklahoma and Texas as the Europeans became dominant. As a youth in Fort Worth, Texas, I was surprised to find that many of my schoolmates were part Native American.

Compare the Beyondist approach to just letting evolution take its course, with many cultures ending by starvation or war.

PREJUDICE

Prejudice is an important topic, from the perspectives of both spirituality and psychology. It is important for spirituality, because, with few exceptions, spirituality seeks to promote ethical treatment of one toward another. It is important to psychology because of its interpersonal impact. But what is prejudice?

EXERCISE

Rate A through I below on the following scales:

Which are they?

Bad 1. 2. 3. 4. 5. Good

Should we allow them to vote?

Definitely No 1. 2. 3. 4. 5. Definitely Yes

Would you recommend hiring them as bank tellers?

Definitely No 1. 2. 3. 4. 5. Definitely Yes

Would you recommend your son or daughter to date and possibly marry one of them?

Definitely No 1. 2. 3. 4. 5. Definitely Yes

A. A person of another race.

B. A person active in your religious faith.

C. A person who actively opposes your religious faith.

D. A divorced person just released from serving a five-year sentence for spouse beating.

E. An escaped criminal wanted for child rape.

F. A pathological liar.

G. A bigot organizing a community to kick out all of the "racially impure."

H. A non-U.S. citizen who plans to return to their home country shortly.

I. A person of your own ethnic subgroup.

Before going on, be sure to rate each category on each scale. Observe how and why you made each decision.

Answers to these questions will vary depending on your assumptions, so no right–wrong scoring key is provided. Your logic is the critical issue.

Prejudice as Stereotypic Prejudgment

Psychologists define prejudice in its most basic form as a "prejudgment or unjustifiable negative attitude" (see Myers, 1993, for an overview). Prejudice is operationalized by measuring "old" or "blatant" prejudice or by measuring "modern" or "subtle" or "new" or "automatic processing" prejudice. Prejudice is always undesirable and a pejorative label in both psychology and spirituality.

Prejudice is a stereotypical prejudgment based on group membership without recognition of the individual's characteristics. It is engaged when a person accepts or rejects individuals solely because of their group membership and ignores or does not seek out information that is more exact. This is in contrast to judging individuals on their own characteristics regardless of group membership. Spirituality supports such definitions and welcomes psychology's knowledge base of when and where stereotyping occurs.

Some of the question–person combinations of the exercise are generally seen as prejudiced by the basic definition of prejudice being prejudgment. Denying a job as a teller to a person of another race based on race alone is seen as prejudgment and therefore prejudice.

The traditional method of operationalizing prejudice is by asking questions about negative and positive attitudes toward a group or by using a measure of social distance. The social distance measure asks whether a group's members should be allowed in the country, allowed to become citizens, and so on to "allowed to be a member of my family by marriage." A social distance measure may be used for one or more groups and for people in general.

The social distance measure allows an interesting check on the definition of prejudice: rating one's own group along with others. Negative attitudes toward one's own group correlate highly with negative attitudes toward others (Boivin, Darling, & Darling, 1987; Teruya, 1996). This suggests that some people are misanthropic; that is, they wish to keep all people at a distance. Misanthropy scales attempt to measure this general negative view of all people directly.

As expected, both social distance of one's own group and misanthropy scales do correlate with scales of prejudice (Teruya, 1996). Thus, one source of high scores on prejudice scales are those people who are negative toward all human groups but may not be particularly biased toward the group being measured over and above that general attitude.

Measurement of blatant forms of prejudice is more difficult now than before the civil rights movement. It is no longer socially correct to admit prejudice by supporting segregation and other such policies. Attempts have been made to measure "modern" prejudice, which is subtle or automatic. "Subtle" prejudice is prejudice in a socially acceptable form and "automatic" is prejudicial action done without awareness. The latter occurs when a person makes a decision based only on group membership without realizing that they are doing so. It is hypothesized to be a function of past learning within a prejudiced subculture.

In addition to the personality characteristic of misanthropy, stereotypic judgments and negative attitudes arise from ethnocentrism found in group membership. As noted previously, each group values itself and its members more highly then other groups even if there is no basis for doing so. Other groups are derogated. This ethnocentric bias is found in every group. The only time it is not found is when there are no identifiable groups. The more group membership is salient or easily observed, the more likely it is that the ethnocentric bias will occur. Hence, we theoretically expect everyone who has a strong group identification to show ethnocentric bias. That would result in higher prejudice scores when rating others not identified with their group. Those who are least prejudiced would be those who are unconnected to any group.

Spirituality should be a prime commitment for everyone. A spiritual commitment is usually accomplished from within a group context, such as a religion. As a prime commitment, it is a strong definer of groups and group boundaries. Therefore, spirituality should be a major source of group identity and the resulting ethnocentric biases.

The prime evidence contrary to the ethnocentric bias interpretation for religions is the finding that the most active Christians are less prejudiced than inactive Christians (Batson & Burris, 1994; Gorsuch & Aleshire, 1974). Since activity is one measure of group identification, the prediction would be that the active Christians would show more ethnocentric bias than inactive Christians would. It is possible that this reversal of prediction is a function of those aspects of Christian theology that stress acceptance of others. In this area, Jesus was a radical. He associated with outcasts whom the community judged as sinners (e.g., the adulterous woman he met at a well; John 4:7) or traitors to their country (the tax collectors for the Roman government, such as

Matthew; Matthew 9:9). Even more radically, he asks us to pray for our enemies and for those who despitefully use us (Matthew 5:44).

A further antiprejudice element of theology is that of "rejecting the sin but not the sinner." Christians attempt to differentiate between the two and act accordingly. When differentiation does occur, individuals are less likely to be stereotypically judged. One must know the person instead of just the group membership.

From a Christian perspective, spirituality needs to be a prime method of offsetting the stereotypical judgments that arise from ethnocentrism and prejudice. Since groups are always forming, and since groups always show ethnocentrism, spirituality will always need to be fighting prejudice from that source.

Prejudice as Negative Attitude

Some authors include more than just stereotyping in definitions of prejudice. They define prejudice as any "intolerant, unfair, unfavorable attitude" (Deaux & Wrightsman, 1988) toward a group and its members. Prejudice is a term that everyone spontaneously knows the meaning of, but the more it is investigated, the more this definition of prejudice becomes problematic.

Further elaboration of the definition of prejudice with other terms requires integration with spirituality. A phrase such as "unjustified negative attitudes" raises the question of why it is felt to be unjustified and by whom. Of course, given our ethnocentric bias, it is always unjustified if it is our group that is under attack and never unjustified if we are attacking another group. Adding to the definition phrases such as "unfair" just adds the same problem again: What group or subculture standard will be used to define "fairness"?

A different problem arises if the definition of prejudice includes "unfavorable attitude." Since prejudice is socially unacceptable, this defines any negative judgment of any group as prejudice. This addition to the definition implies that either there are no differences between groups (since someone might see that difference as favoring one or the other group) or that we should pretend there are no differences between groups. Is a negative attitude toward a category of war criminals prejudice? Or is it an appropriate response to their crimes?

The point missed by defining prejudice as "negative attitudes" is, from a spirituality perspective, that decisions must be made and that such decisions must include a value base. That base is provided by one's ethics. In ethics there are those who are more ethical and those who are less. The more ethical need to be distinguished from the less ethical and responded to accordingly. Hence, groups are always involved, at least implicitly, and some groups must be judged less desirable than others are judged.

The problem of defining prejudice continues in some modern scales. For example, Pettigrew and Meertens (1995) score a person as having subtle prejudice if they believe another group has a religion different than their own or speaks another language. In their research on views of immigrants to England from countries such as India, it appears that anyone knowing that the group really did have another religion or language would be labeled prejudiced, whereas those ignorant of the information would be rated nonprejudiced!

The earlier exercise contained several groups that are judged different ways depending on the spirituality of the judge. In the U.S. tradition of democracy, any denial of voting rights is considered prejudice. Griffen, Gorsuch, and Davis (1987) used this and other civil rights as a measure of prejudice when two religious groups were competing in the recruitment of the same people. But even democracy has limits on acceptance of all people. The exercise contains two categories of people not allowed to vote: criminals and citizens of another country.

Who would be the person who answered three to all the ratings in the exercise? One such person would say that we had insufficient evidence in all those cases to reach a decision. Such a rationale is difficult, given that voting is defined by law and noncitizens are not allowed to vote.

But other people answering three to all the ratings would be those who have given up all judgments of other people. To carry this to the logical conclusion is to say that we should accept all behaviors of all people no matter how much those behaviors hurt another person. In that case bigots should be just as acceptable as are people from other races as are child rapists as are our best friends. Some types of spirituality could go so far as to say that none should ever make judgments about others, but that is rare in theory and impossible in practice.

For spirituality, decisions about others are necessary and good. Hence, expanding the definition of prejudice to include any and all negative attitudes is inappropriate. But to define prejudice more appropriately is a high priority.

The Next Steps

There is one aspect that spirituality lifts up for social psychology's attention: the need for ways of reducing prejudice, including through spirituality. Despite over four decades of research on prejudice, including the relationship of Christianity to prejudice, experimental studies are almost nonexistent except for Rokeach (1975) and a couple of follow-up studies (Altemeyer, 1994; Oordt, 1991).

The most common situation for exploring interventions to reduce prejudice has been in schools, out of a need to identify the effects on school integration (Stephan & Stephan, 2001). While work such as that by Stephan and Stephan is excellent, it is curious that "spirituality," "religion," or even "democracy" are not in the index. The only place values are mentioned is when they are without content. It is clear that the book assumes that conflict between U.S. subcultures is to be avoided, as are policies and practices that produce a more negative impact upon one group than another. However, without a spirituality involvement, the assumptions are only unsupported assumptions, and the students' spiritualities are not directly engaged to reduce prejudice.

If we really are against prejudice, it is past time to investigate ways spirituality can reduce prejudice. Church groups have long had programs to reduce prejudice, but psychologists seldom cooperate with church groups for field research. Nor have psychologists developed sufficient research programs of their own to find out how to reduce prejudice. Such programs can only happen when spirituality and psychology form an integrated approach to reducing prejudice.

CHAPTER 7

Epilogue

Having come this far, what can we conclude? That is a matter for you to decide. In the final analysis, integration is personal. Here are some conclusions I hope you can support:

- Integration can be fascinating.
- Integration is necessary. We already do it, so let's do it well.
- Uninformed integration is as valuable as most other uninformed activities.
- If you wish to formally integrate two disciplines, study both but be a slave to neither. Or collaborate in dialogue with a person from another discipline.
- Integration can be helped by dialogue. I have learned much from others, and hope my sharing via this book has stimulated you.
- Each new generation will do integration better as it stand on the shoulders of those who have gone before—provided they read those who have gone before.

The only true epilogue is what you do with integration in your life.

References

Adams, J. (1986). *The biblical view of self-esteem, self-love, self-image*. Eugene, OR: Harvest House.

Ajzen, I. (1988). *Attitudes, personality, and behavior*. Chicago: Dorsey Press.

Ajzen, I., & Fishbein, M. (1980). *Understanding attitudes and predicting social behavior*. Englewood Cliffs, NJ: Prentice Hall.

Allport, G. W., & Ross, J. M. (1967). Personal religious orientation and prejudice. *Journal of Personality and Social Psychology, 5*, 432–443.

Altemeyer, B. (1994). Reducing prejudice in right-wing authoritarians. In M. P. Zanna & J. M. Olson (Eds.), *The psychology of prejudice* (pp. 131–148). Hillsdale, NJ: Lawrence Erlbaum.

Aquinas, T. (1990). The Summa Theologica. In M. J. Adler (Ed.), *Great books of the Western world: Vol. 30*. Chicago: Encyclopaedia Britannica.

Aristotle. (345 B.C./1990). Bhysics: Book II. In M. J. Adler (Ed.), *Great books of the Western world*. Chicago: Encyclopaedia Britannica.

Augsburger, David W. (1994). *Conflict mediation across cultures*. Louisville, KY: Westminster John Knox Press.

Augustine. (400/1990). Confessions. In M. J. Adler (Ed.), *Great books of the Western world: Vol. 16* (pp. 1–159). Chicago: Encyclopaedia Britannica.

Axelrod, R. (1980). More effective choice in the prisoner's dilemma. *Journal of Conflict Resolution, 24*, 379–403.

Bar-Tel, D., & Kruglanski, A. W. (Eds.). (1988). *The social psychology of knowledge*. New York: Cambridge University Press.

Batson, C. D. (1976). Religion as prosocial: Agent or double agent? *Journal for the scientific study of religion, 15* (1), 29–45.

Batson, C. D., & Burris, C. T. (1994). Personal religion: Depressant or stimulant of prejudice and discrimination? In M. P. Zanna & J. M. Olson (Eds.), *The psychology of prejudice* (pp. 149–170). Hillsdale, NJ: Lawrence Erlbaum.

Batson, C. D., & Schoenrade, D. A. (1991). Measuring religion as quest: Validity concerns. *Journal for the Scientific Study of Religion, 30* (4), 416–429.

Batson, C. D., & Ventis, L. (1993). *Religion and the individual: A social–psychological perspective.* New York: Oxford University Press.

Baumeister, R. F. (1997). *Evil: Inside human cruelty and violence.* New York: W. H. Freeman.

Bergin, A. E. (1991). Values and religious issues in psychotherapy and mental health. *American Psychologist, 46,* 1–8.

Bergin, A. E. & Payne, I. R. (1991). Proposed agenda for a spiritual strategy in personality and psychotherapy. *Journal of Psychology and Christianity, 10,* 197–210.

Bjorck, J. P. (1993). Coping with threats, losses, and challenges. *Journal of Social and Clinical Psychology, 12* (1), 56–72.

Blackmore, S. J. (1996). *In search of the light: The adventures of a parapsychologist.* Amherst, NY: Prometheus Books.

Boisen, A. (1936). *The exploration of the inner world: A study of mental disorder and religious experience.* New York: Harper and Brothers.

Boivin, M. J., Darling, H. W., & Darling, T. W. (1987). Racial prejudice among Christian and non-Christian college students. *Journal of Psychology and Theology, 15* (1), 45–56.

Boorstin, D. J. (1983). *The discoverers.* New York: Vintage Books.

Bradley, K. (1996). Two "cop-outs" in faith-learning integration: Incarnational integration and worldviewish integration. *Spectrum, 28*(2), 105–118.

Bronfrenbrenner, U. (1970). *Two worlds of childhood: U.S. and U.S.S.R.* New York: Russell Sage Foundation.

Brown, C. (1968). *Philosophy and the Christian faith.* Downers Grove, IL: InterVarsity Press.

Brown, C. (1985). *That you may believe: Miracles and faith then and now.* Grand Rapids, MI: William B. Eerdmans.

Brown, H.O.J. (1991). The Crusade or preventive war. In R. G. Clouse (Ed.), *War: Four Christian views* (pp. 151–168). Downers Grove, IL: InterVarsity Press.

Brown, R. (1995). *Prejudice: Its social psychology.* Cambridge, MA: Blackwell.

Brown, W. S., Murphy, N. C., & Malony, H. N. (1998). *Whatever happened to the soul? Scientific and theological portraits of the soul.* Minneapolis, MN: Fortress Press.

Browning, D. S. (1987). *Religious thought and the modern psychologies.* Philadelphia, PA: Fortress.

Bufford, R. K. (1997). Consecrated counseling: Reflections on the distinctives of Christian counseling. *Journal of Psychology and Theology, 25,* 110–121.

Bull, N. J. (1969). *Moral judgment from childhood to adolescence.* Beverly Hills, CA: Sage.

Campbell, A. (1835/1975). *The Christian system.* North Stratford: Ayer.

Campbell, D. T., & Stanley, J. C. (1963). *Experimental and quasi-experimental designs for research.* Boston: Houghton Mifflin.

Carter, J. D. (1977). Secular and sacred models of psychology and religion. *Journal of Psychology and Theology, 5,* 197–208.

Carter, J. D., & Mohline, R. J. (1976). The nature and scope of integration: A proposal. *Journal of Psychology and Theology, 4,* 3–14.

Cattell, R. B. (1965). *The scientific analysis of personality*. Baltimore: Penguin Books.

Cattell, R. B. (1972). *A new morality from science: Beyondism*. New York: Pergamon.

Cattell, R. B. (1987). *Beyondism: Religion from science*. New York: Praeger.

Cattell, R. B., & Child, D. (1975). *Motivation and dynamic structure*. New York: Halsted (Wiley).

Clayton, P. (1989). *Explanation from physics to theology*. New Haven, CT: Yale University Press.

Clayton, P. (1997). *God and contemporary science*. Grand Rapids, MI: William B. Eerdmans.

Clouse, R. G. (1991). *War: Four Christian views*. Downers Grove, IL: InterVarsity Press.

Cohen, J., & Cohen, P. (1983). *Applied multiple regression/correlation analysis for the behavioral sciences* (2d ed.). Hillsdale, NJ: Lawrence Erlbaum.

Cole, B. S., & Pargament, K. I. (1999). Spiritual surrender: A paradoxical path to control. In W. R. Miller (Ed.), *Integrating spirituality into treatment: Resources for practitioners* (pp. 179–198). Washington, DC: American Psychological Association.

Collins, G. (1980). *Christian counseling: A comprehensive guide*. Waco, TX: Word.

Connors, G. J., Toscova, R. T., & Tonigan, J. S. (1999). Serenity. In W. R. Miller (Ed.), *Integrating spirituality into treatment: Resources for practitioners* (pp. 235–250). Washington, DC: American Psychological Association.

Cosgrove, M., & Mallory, J. (1977). *Mental Health: A Christian perspective*. Grand Rapids, MI: Zondervan.

Crabb, L. J., Jr. (1977). *Effective biblical counseling: A model of helping caring Christians become capable counselors*. Grand Rapids, MI: Zondervan.

Damasio, A. R. (1994). *Descartes' error: Emotion, reason, and the human brain*. New York: G. P. Putnam's Sons.

Darley, J. M., Glucksberg, S., & Kinchla, R. A. (1988). *Psychology* (4th ed.). Englewood Cliffs, NJ: Prentice Hall.

Davis, E. (1996). Newton's rejection of the "Newtonian world view." In Jitse M. van der Meer (Ed.), *Facets of faith and science, vol. 3, The role of beliefs in the natural sciences* (pp. 75–96). Lantham, MD: University Press of America.

Deaux, K., & Wrightsman, L. S. (1988). *Social psychology*. Pacific Grove, CA: Brooks/Cole.

Descartes, R. (1701/1990). Discourse on the method of rightly conducting the reason. In P. W. Goetz, (Ed.) *Great books of the Western world: Vol. 28* (pp. 263–291, 2d ed.). Chicago: Encyclopaedia Britannica.

Du Casse, C. J. (1969). *Causation and the types of necessity*. New York: Dover.

Dueck, A. C. (1995) Between Jerusalem and Athens. Grand Rapids, MI Baker Books.

Eck, B. E. (1996). Integrating the integrators: An organizing framework for a multifaceted process of integration. *Journal of Psychology and Christianity, 15,* 101–115.

Ellens, J. H. (1982). *God's grace and human health*. Nashville, TN: Abingdon.

Ellison, C. (1994). *From stress to well-being*. Dallas, TX: Word.

Enright, R. D., & The Human Development Study Group. (1996). Counseling within the forgiveness triad: On forgiving, receiving forgiveness, and self-forgiveness. *Counseling and Values, 40,* 107–126.

Farnsworth, K. E. (1985). *Wholehearted integration: Harmonizing psychology and Christianity through word and deed.* Grand Rapids, MI: Baker Books.

Faw, Harold W. (1995). *Psychology in Christian perspective.* Grand Rapids, MI: Baker Books.

Finney, J. R., & Malony, H. N. (1985a). Contemplative prayer and its use in psychotherapy: A theoretical model. *Journal of Psychology and Theology, 13,* 172–181.

Finney, J. R., & Malony, H. N. (1985b). Empirical studies of Christian prayer: A review of the literature. *Journal of Psychology and Theology, 13,* 104–115.

Finney, J. R., & Malony, H. N. (1985c). An empirical study of contemplative prayer as an adjunct to psychotherapy. *Journal of Psychology and Theology, 13,* 284–290.

Fleck, J. R., & Carter, J. D. (1981). *Psychology and Christianity: Integrative readings.* Nashville, TN: Abingdon.

Francis, L. J., & Jones, S. H. (1996). *Psychological perspectives on Christian ministry.* Herefordshire, England: Gracewing.

Freud, S. (1927/1964). *The future of an illusion* (Rev. ed.). Garden City, NJ: Doubleday.

Friedlander, M. W. (1995). *At the fringes of science.* San Fransisco: Westview Press.

Fulton, A. S., Gorsuch, R. L., & Maynard, E. A. (1999). Religious orientation, antihomosexual sentiment, and fundamentalism among Christians. *Journal for the Scientific Study of Religion, 38,* 14–22.

Funk, R. W. (1982). *Parables and presence: Forms of the New Testament tradition.* Philadelphia, PA: Fortress Press.

Funk, R. W., & the Jesus Seminar. (1998). *The acts of Jesus: The search for the authentic deeds of Jesus.* San Francisco: Polebridge Press.

Garner, D. M., & Garfinkel, P. E. (Eds.). (1997). *Handbook for treatment of eating disorders.* New York: Guilford Press.

Gibbon, E. (1776/1990). *The decline and fall of the Roman empire, Vol. 1.* In M. J. Adler (Ed.), *Great books of the Western world: Vol. 37* (p. 8, 2d ed.). Chicago: Encyclopaedia Britannica.

Gilligan, C. (Ed.). (1988). *Mapping the moral domain: A contribution of women's thinking to psychological theory and education.* Cambridge: Harvard University Press.

Goetz, P. W. (Ed.). (1990). *Great books of the Western world* (2d ed.). Chicago: Encyclopaedia Britannica.

Gorsuch, R. L. (1983). *Factor analysis* (2d ed.). Hillsdale, NJ: Lawrence Erlbaum.

Gorsuch, R. L. (1984). Measurement: The boon and bane of investigating religion. *American Psychologist, 39* (3), 228–236.

Gorsuch, R. L. (1986). Psychology and religion, beliefs, and values. *Journal of Psychology and Christianity, 5* (2), 38–44.

Gorsuch, R. L. (1988). Psychology of religion. In M. R. Rosenzweig & L. W. Porter (Eds.), *Annual review of psychology, vol. 39* (pp. 201–221). Palo Alto, CA: Annual Reviews.

Gorsuch, R. L. (1990–1999). *UniMult: For univariate and multivariate data analysis.* (Computer program and guide). Pasadena, CA: UniMult.

Gorsuch, R. L. (1993). Assessing spiritual variables in Alcoholics Anonymous. In B. S. McCrady & W. R. Miller (Eds.), *Research on Alcoholics Anony-*

mous: Opportunities and alternatives (pp. 301–318). New Brunswick, NJ: Rutgers Center of Alcohol Studies.

Gorsuch, R. L. (1995). Religious aspects of substance abuse and recovery. *Journal of Social Issues, 51* (2), 65–83.

Gorsuch, R. L., & Aleshire, D. (1974). Christian faith and ethnic prejudice: A review and interpretation of research. *Journal for the Scientific Study of Religion, 13,* 281–307.

Gorsuch, R. L., & Barnes, M. L. (1973). Stages of ethical reasoning and moral norms of Carib youths. *Journal of Cross-Cultural Psychology, 4,* 283–301.

Gorsuch, R. L., Friesen, D., & Robert, L. (1998, November). *Intrinsic and extrinsic religious motivation across cultures.* Paper presented at the Society for the Scientific Study of Religion/Religious Research Association Annual Meeting, Montreal, Canada.

Gorsuch, R. L., & Leung, A. (1991, August). *Intervention to facilitate use of psychological services by Chinese Americans.* Paper presented at the Annual Convention of the American Psychological Association, San Fransisco, CA.

Gorsuch, R. L., & Malony, H. N. (1976). *The nature of man: A social psychological perspective.* Springfield, IL: Charles C. Thomas.

Gorsuch, R. L., & McPherson, S. E. (1989). Intrinsic/extrinsic measurment: I/E revised and single-item scales. *Journal for the Scientific Study of Religion, 28* (3), 348–354.

Gorsuch, R. L., & Meylink, W. D. (1988). Toward a co-professional model of clergy–psychologist referral. *Journal of Psychology and Christianity, 7* (3), 22–31.

Gorsuch, R. L., Ortberg, J. C., Jr., & Kim, G. (2001). Changing attitude and moral obligation: Their differential effects on behavior. *Journal for the Scientific Study of Religion, 40* (3), 489–496.

Gorsuch, R. L., & Smith, C. S. (1983). Attributions of responsibility to God: A function of religious beliefs. *Journal for the Scientific Study of Religion, 22,* 340–352.

Gorsuch, R. L., & Smith, R. A. (1972). Changes in college students' evaluations of moral behavior: 1969 versus 1939, 1949, and 1958. *Journal of Psychology and Social Psychology, 24* (3), 381–391.

Gorsuch, R. L., & Spilka, B. (1987). Retrospective review: The varieties in historical and contemporary contexts. *Contemporary Psychology, 32,* 773–778.

Griffen, G.A.E., Gorsuch, R. L., & Davis, A. (1987). A cross-cultural investigation of religious orientation, social norms, and prejudice. *Journal for the Scientific Study of Religion, 26* (3), 358–365.

Griffioen, S. (1989). The worldview approach to social theory: Hazards and benefits. In P. A. Marshall, S. Griffioen, & R. J. Mouw (Eds.), *Stained glass: Worldviews and social science* (pp. 81–118). New York: University Press.

Hao, J. Y. (1993). *Religious beliefs, affects, and values toward supporting women's pastoral leadership: Applying reasoned action and aggregation theories.* Unpublished doctoral dissertation, Fuller Theological Seminary, Pasadena, CA.

Hao, J. Y., & Gorsuch, R. L. (1993). Forgiveness: An exploratory factor analysis and its relationship to religious variables. *Review of Religious Research, 34,* 333–347.

Harding, R. (1992). *The Bible and counseling*. London: Hodder and Stoughton.

Hart, A. (1998). *Secrets of Eve: Understanding the mystery of female sexuality*. Nashville: Word.

Hill, P., & Butter, E. M. (1995). The role of religion in promoting physical health. *Journal of Psychology & Christianity, 14* (2), 141–155.

Holmes, A. F. (1991). The just war. In R. G. Clouse (Ed.), *War: Four Christian views*. Downers Grove, IL: InterVarsity Press.

Homer. (700 B.C./1951). *The Iliad* (R. Lattimore, Trans.). In M. J. Adler (Ed.). (1990). *Great books of the Western world: Vol. 3* (2d ed.). Chicago: Encyclopaedia Britannica.

Hood, R. W., Jr., Spilka, B., Hunsberger, B., & Gorsuch, R. L. (1996). *The psychology of religion: An empirical approach* (2d ed.). New York: Guilford Press.

Hood, R. W., Jr., Spilka, B., Hunsberger, B., & Gorsuch, R. L. (in press). *The psychology of religion: An empirical approach* (3d ed.). New York: Guilford Press.

Hoshmand, L. T. (Ed.). (1998). *Creativity and moral vision in psychology*. Thousand Oaks, CA: Sage.

Howard, G. S. (1993). On certain blindnesses in human beings: Psychology and world overpopulation. *Counseling Psychologist, 21*, 560–581.

Hunsberger, B. (1996). Religious fundamentalism, right-wing authoritarianism and hostility toward homosexuals in non-Christian religious groups. *International Journal for the Psychology of Religion, 6*, 39–49.

Hunt, R. A. (1991). *The psychology of clergy*. Harrisburg, PA: Morehouse Publishing.

Hunt, R. A., & Hunt, J.A.F. (1994). *Awaken your power to love*. Nashville, TN: T. Nelson.

Jessor, R., Graves, T. D., Hanson, R. C., & Jessor, S. L. (1968). *Society, personality, and deviant behavior: A study of a tri-ethnic community*. New York: Holt, Rinehart, and Winston.

Johnson, C. (1983). *The psychology of Biblical interpretation*. Grand Rapids, MI: Zondervan.

Johnston, D., & Sampson, C. (1994). *Religion, the missing dimension of statecraft*. New York: Oxford University Press.

Jones, S. L. (Ed.). (1986a). *Psychology and the Christian faith: An introductory reader*. Grand Rapids, MI: Baker Book House.

Jones, S. L. (1986b). Relating the Christian faith to psychology. In S. L. Jones (Ed.), *Psychology and the Christian faith: An introductory reader* (pp. 15–34). Grand Rapids, MI: Baker Book House.

Jones, S. L. (1994). A constructive relationship for religion with the science and profession of psychology: Perhaps the boldest model yet. *American Psychologist, 49*, 184–199.

Jones, S. L., & Buttman, R. E. (1991). *Modern psychotherapies: A comprehensive Christian appraisal*. Downers Grove, IL: InterVarsity Press.

Kohlberg, L. (1969). Stage and sequence: The cognitive–developmental approach to socialization. In D. A. Goslin (Ed.), *Handbook of socialization theory and research* (pp. 347–480). Chicago: Rand McNally.

Kooistra, J. D. (1997). Paradigm shifty things. *Analog, 67* (6), 59–69.

Kuhn, T. S. (1970). *The structure of scientific revolutions* (2d ed.). Chicago: University of Chicago Press.

Kurtz, P., & Fraknoi, A. (1996). Scientific tests of astrology do not support its claims. In J. Nickell, B. Kerr, & T. Genoni (Eds.), *The outer edge*. Amherst, NY: Committee for the Scientific Investigations of the Claims of the Paranormal.

Larson, D. B., & Larson, S. S. (1994). *The forgotten factor in physical and mental health: What does the research show? An independent study seminar*. Bethesda, MD: David and Susan Larson.

Larzelere, R. E. (1980). The task ahead: Six levels of integration of Christianity and psychology. *Journal of Psychology and Theology, 8*, 3–11.

Lawrence, Brother. (1974). *The practice of the presence of God* (D. Atwater, Trans.). Springfield, IL: Templegate.

Leung, W. Y. (1991). *Intervention to facilitate use of psychological services by Chinese Americans*. Unpublished master's thesis, Fuller Theological Seminary, Pasadena, CA.

Lovinger, R. J. (1984). *Working with religious issues in therapy*. New York: Jason Aronson.

Lovinger, R. J. (1990). *Religion and counseling: The psychological impact of religious belief*. New York: Continuum.

Lovinger, R. J. (1996). Considering the religious dimension in assessment and treatment. In E. P. Shafranske (Ed.), *Religion and the clinical practice of psychology* (pp. 327–364). Washington, DC: American Psychological Association.

MacNutt, F. (1995). *Deliverance from evil spirits*. Grand Rapids, MI: Chosen Books.

Malony, H. N. (Ed.). (1978). *Psychology and faith: The Christian experience of eighteen psychologists*. Washington, DC: University Press of America.

Malony, H. N. (1983). *Wholeness and holiness: Readings in the pychology and theology of mental health*. Grand Rapids, MI: Baker Books.

Malony, H. N. (1988). The clinical assessment of optimal religious functioning. *Review of Religious Research, 30* (1), 3–17.

Malony, H. N. (1995a). *The psychology of religion for ministry*. Mahwah, NJ: Paulist Press.

Malony, H. N. (1995b). *Win–win relationships: Nine strategies for settling personal conflicts without waging war*. Nashville, TN: Broadman and Holman.

Marlatt, G. A., & Kristeller, J. L. (1999). Mindfulness and meditation. In W. R. Miller (Ed.), *Integrating spirituality into treatment: Resources for practitioners* (pp. 67–84). Washington, DC: American Psychological Association.

Marshall, P. A., Griffioen, S., & Mouw, R. J. (Eds.). (1989). *Stained glass: Worldviews and social science*. New York: University Press.

Martin, J. E., & Booth, J. (1999). Behavioral approaches to enhance spirituality. In W. R. Miller (Ed.), *Integrating spirituality into treatment: Resources for practitioners*. Washington, DC: American Psychological Association.

McCullough, M. E., & Larson, D. B. (1999) Prayer. In W. R. Miller (Ed.), *Integrating spirituality into treatment: Resources for practitioners* (pp. 85–110). Washington, DC: American Psychological Association.

McCullough, M. E., Worthington, E. L., & Rachal, K. C. (1997). Interpersonal forgiving in close relationships. *Journal of Personality and Social Psychology, 73*, 321–336.

McDonald, H. D. (1986). Biblical teaching on personality. In S. L. Jones (Ed.), *Psychology and the Christian faith: An introductory reader* (pp. 118–140). Grand Rapids, MI: Baker Book House.

McDougall, W. (1908). *An introduction to social psychology*. London: Methuen.

McLemore, C. (1982). *The scandal of psychotherapy*. Wheaton, IL: Tyndale.

McMinn, M. R. (1996). *Psychology, theology, and spirituality in Christian counseling*. Wheaton, IL: Tyndale House.

Mebane, D. L., & Ridley, C. R. (1988). The role-sending of perfectionism: Overcoming counterfeit spirituality. *Journal of Psychology and Theology, 16*, 332–339.

Meek, K. R., & McMinn, M. R. (1997). Forgiveness: More than a psychotherapeutic technique. *Journal of Psychology and Christianity, 16*, 51–61.

Meier, R., Minirth, F., Wichern, F., & Ratcliff, E. (1991). *Introduction to psychology and counseling*. Grand Rapids, MI: Baker Books.

Meyers, D. (1999). *Social psychology*. Boston: McGraw-Hill.

Meylink, W. D., & Gorsuch, R. L. (1986a). Clergy–psychologist referrals: Toward a model of cooperation. In H. N. Malony (Ed.), *Is there a shrink in the Lord's house: How psychologists can help the church* (pp. 189–199). Pasadena, CA: Integration Press.

Meylink, W. D., & Gorsuch, R. L. (1986b). New perspectives for clergy psychologist referrals. *Journal of Psychology and Christianity, 5* (3), 62–70.

Meylink, W. D., & Gorsuch, R. L. (1987). Two-way referrals in clergy–psychologist relations. *International Christian Digest, 1* (6), 20–21.

Meylink, W. D., & Gorsuch, R. L. (1988). Relationship between clergy and psychologists: The empirical data. *Journal of Psychology and Christianity, 7* (1), 56–72.

Milgram, S. (1974). *Obedience to authority*. New York: Harper and Row.

Miller, G. A. (1956). The magical number seven, plus or minus two. *Psychological Review, 63*, 81–97.

Miller, W. R. (1988). Including clients' spiritual perspectives in cognitive behavior therapy with religious clients. In W. R. Miller & J. E. Martins (Eds.), *Behavior therapy and religion: Integrating spiritual and behavioral approaches to change* (pp. 43–55). Newbury Park, CA: Sage.

Miller, W. R. (1999). *Integrating spirituality into treatment: Resources for practitioners*. Washington, DC: American Psychological Association.

Miller, W. R., & Martins, J. E. (Eds.). (1988). *Behavior therapy and religion: Integrating spiritual and behavioral approaches to change*. Newbury Park, CA: Sage.

Mouw, R. J. (1992). *Uncommon decency: Christian civility in an uncivil world*. Downers Grove, IL: InterVarsity Press.

Mowrer, O. H. (1961). *The crisis in psychiatry and religion*. Princeton, NJ: Van Nostrand.

Murphy, N. (1990). *Theology in the age of scientific reasoning*. New York: Cornell University Press.

Murphy, N. (1995). Divine action in the natural order: Buridan's ass and Schrodinger's cat. In R. J. Russell, N. Murphy, & A. R. Peacocke (Eds.), *Chaos and complexity: Scientific perspectives on divine action*. Berkeley, CA: Center for Theology and the Natural Sciences.

Murphy, N. (1997). *Anglo-American postmodernity*. Boulder, CO: Westview Press.

Myers, D. G. (1986). Social psychology. In S. L. Jones (Ed.), *Psychology and the Christian faith: An introductory reader* (pp. 217–239). Grand Rapids, MI: Baker Book House.

Myers, D. G. (1994). *Social psychology*. New York: McGraw-Hill.

Newton, I. (1726/1990). Mathematical principles of natural philosophy. In P. W. Goetz (Ed.). (1990), *Great books of the Western world: Vol. 32* (pp. 1–372, 2d ed.). Chicago: Encyclopaedia Britannica.

Niebuhr, H. R. (1956). *Christ and culture*. New York: Harper and Brothers.

Niven, L., & Pournelle, J. (1993). *The gripping hand*. New York: Pocket Books.

Nunnally, J. C., & Bernstein, I. H. (1994). *Psychometric theory* (3d ed.). New York: McGraw-Hill.

O'Donohue, W., & Kitchner, R. E. (Eds.). (1996). *The philosophy of psychology*. Thousand Oaks, CA: Sage.

Oordt, M. S. (1991). *Value change, authority, and religious tolerance: A re-examination of the cognitive consistency model*. Unpublished doctoral dissertation, Fuller Theological Seminary, Pasadena, CA.

Orkin, M. (1999). *What are the odds? Chance in everyday life*. New York: W. H. Freeman.

Ortberg, J. C., Jr., Gorsuch, R. L., & Kim, G. J. (2001). Changing attitude and moral obligation: Their independent effects on behavior. *Journal for the Scientific Study of Religion, 40*, 489–496.

Paluzian, R. F. (1996). *Invitation to the psychology of religion* (2d ed.). Boston: Allyn and Bacon.

Pargament, K. I. (1997). *The psychology of religion and coping: Theory, research, practice*. New York: Guilford Press.

Pascal, B. (1670/1990). *Pensées* (W. F. Trotter, Trans.). In M. J. Adler (Ed.), *Great books of the Western world: Vol. 30* (2d ed.). Chicago: Encylopaedia Britannica.

Payne, I., Bergin, A. E., Bielema, K. A., & Jenkins, P. H. (1991). Review of religion and mental health: Prevention and the enhancement of psychological functioning. *Prevention in Human Services, 9*(2), 11–40.

Payne, I., Bergin, A. E., & Loftus, P. E. (1992). A review of attempts to integrate spiritual and standard psychotherapy techniques. *Journal of Psychotherapy Integration, 2* (3), 171–192.

Peacocke, A. (1993). *Theology for a scientific age: Being and becoming—natural, divine and human*. Minneapolis, MN: Fortress Press.

Peck, R. F., & Havinghurst, R. T. (1960). *Psychology of character development*. New York: Wiley.

Pettigrew, T. F., & Meertens, R. W. (1995). Subtle and blatant prejudice in Western Europe. In E. Aronson (Ed.), *Readings about the social animal* (pp. 443–460). New York: Freeman.

Propst, L. R. (1988). *Psychotherapy in a religious framework: Spirituality in the emotional healing process*. New York: Human Sciences Press.

Raloff, J. (1988). Nutrition. *Science News, 126*, 351.

Richards, J. S., Rector, J. M., & Tjelveit, A. (1999). Values, spirituality, and psychotherapy. In W. R. Miller (Ed.), *Integrating spirituality into treatment: Resources for practitioners* (pp. 133–160). Washington, DC: American Psychological Association.

Richards, P. S., & Bergin, A. E. (Eds.). (1997). *A spiritual strategy for counseling and psychotherapy*. Washington, DC: American Psychological Association.

Ring, K. (1980). *Life at death: A scientific investigation of the near-death experience*. New York: Coward, McCann, and Geoghegan.

Rokeach, M. (1975). Long-term value change initiated by computer feedback. *Journal of Personality and Social Psychology, 32,* 467–476.

Rosenhan, D. L., & London, P. (1975). *Theory and research in abnormal psychology* (2d ed.). New York: Holt, Rinehart, and Winston.

Russell, R. J. (1995). Introduction. In R. J. Russell, N. Murphy, & A. R. Peacocke (Eds.), *Chaos and complexity: Scientific perspectives on divine action*. Berkeley, CA: Center for Theology and the Natural Sciences.

Russell, R. J., Murphy, N., & Peacocke, A. R. (Eds.). (1995). *Chaos and complexity: Scientific perspectives on divine action*. Berkeley, CA: Center for Theology and the Natural Sciences.

Sanders, R. K. (Ed.). (1997). *Christian counseling ethics: A handbook for therapists, pastors, & counselors*. Downers Grove, IL: InterVarsity Press.

Sanderson, C., & Linehan, M. M. (1999). Acceptance and forgiveness. In W. R. Miller (Ed.), *Integrating spirituality into treatment: Resources for practitioners* (pp. 199–216). Washington, DC: American Psychological Association.

Schaefer, C. A., & Gorsuch, R. L. (1992). Dimensionality of religion: Belief and motivation as predictors of behavior. *Journal of Psychology and Christianity, 11,* 244–254.

Seamands, D. A. (1985). *Healing of memories*. Colorado Springs: Chariot Victor.

Shadish, W. R., & Fuller, S. (1994). *The social psychology of science*. New York: Guilford Press.

Shafranske, E. P., & Gorsuch, R. L. (1984). Factors associated with the perception of spirituality in psychotherapy. *Journal of Transpersonal Psychology, 16,* 231–241.

Shafranske, E. P., & Malony, H. N. (1996). Religion and the clinical practice of psychology: A case for inclusion. In E. P. Shafranske (Ed.), *Religion and the clinical practice of psychology* (pp. 561–586). Washington, DC: American Psychological Association.

Sherif, M., Harvey, O. J., White, B. J., Hood, W. R., & Sherif, C. W. (1961). *Intergroup conflict and cooperation: The Robbers Cave experiment*. Tulsa: University of Oklahoma, Institute of Group Relations.

Sherif, M., & Sherif, C. W. (1969). *Social psychology* (Rev. ed.). New York: Harper and Row.

Shytov, A. N. (2000). *Conscience in making judicial decisions*. Unpublished doctoral dissertation, University of Glasgow.

Simpson, T. K. (1992). Science as mystery: A speculative reading of Newton's *Principia*. In M. J. Adler (Ed.), *The great ideas today*. Chicago: Encyclopaedia Britannica.

Skinner, B. F. (1976). *Walden two*. New York: Macmillan.

Slack, P. (1985). *The impact of plague in Tudor and Stuart England*. London: Routledge and Kegan Paul.

Smith, C. S., & Gorsuch, R. L. (1989). Sanctioning and causal attributions to God: A function of theological position and actors' characteristics. In M. L. Lynn & D. O. Moberg (Eds.), *Research in the social scientific study of religion: A research annual, vol. 1*. Greenwich, CT: JAI Press.

Smith, S. L., & Donnerstein, E. (1998). Harmful effects of exposure to media violence: Learning of aggression, emotional desensitization, and fear. In R. G. Green & E. Donnerstein (Eds.), *Human aggression: Theories, research, and implications for social policy*. San Diego: Academic Press.

Snook, S. C., & Gorsuch, R. L. (1985, August). *Religious orientation and racial prejudice in South Africa*. Paper presented at the 93rd Annual Convention of the American Psychological Association, Los Angeles, CA.

Sorenson, R. L. (1994a). Sea changes, interesting complements and proselytizing in psychoanalysis: Commentary on "An interesting contradiction: A study of religiously committed, psychoanalytically oriented clinicians." *Journal of Psychology and Theology, 22*, 319–321.

Sorenson, R. L. (1994b). Therapists' (and their therapists') God representations in clinical practice. *Journal of Psychology and Theology, 22*, 325–344.

Sorenson, R. L. (1997). Transcendence and intersubjectivity: The patient's experience of the analyst's spirituality. In C. Spezzano et al. (Eds.), *Soul on the couch: Spirituality, religion, and morality in contemporary psychoanalysis* (p. 241). Hillsdale, NJ: Analytic Press.

Southard, S. (1972). *Christians and mental health*. Nashville, TN: Boardman.

Southard, S. (1989). *Theology and therapy*. Dallas, TX: Word.

Spilka, B., & Bridges, R. A. (1989). Theological and psychological theory: Psychological implications for some modern theologies. *Journal of Psychology and Theology, 17*, 343–351.

Stassen, G. H. (1992). *Just peacemaking*. Louisville, KY: Westminster/John Knox Press.

Steele, L. (1986). Developmental psychology and spiritual development. In S. L. Jones (Ed.), *Psychology and the Christian faith: An introductory reader* (pp. 95–117). Grand Rapids, MI: Baker Book House.

Stephan, W. G., & Stephan, C. W. (2001). *Improving intergroup relations*. Thousand Oaks, CA: Sage.

Stern, E. M. (Ed.). (1985). *Psychotherapy and the religiously committed patient*. New York: Hayworth.

Stroud, T. (1973). *Services for children and their families*. Elkins Park, IL: Franklin Book Company.

Tajfel, H. (1981). *Human groups and social categories*. Cambridge: Cambridge University Press.

Tan, S.-Y. (1991). *Lay counseling: Equipping Christians for a helping ministry*. Grand Rapids, MI: Zondervan.

Tan, S.-Y. (1996). Religion in clinical practice: Implicit and explicit integration. In E. Shafranske (Ed.), *Religion and the clinical practice of psychology* (pp. 71–112). Washington, DC: American Psychological Association.

Tan, S.-Y. (1997). *Power connectors: How to connect to the Spirit's power and presence*. Grand Rapids, MI: Zondervan.

Templeton, J. M. (1995). *The humble approach* (Rev. ed.). New York: Continuum.

Templeton, J. M. (1997). *How large is God?* Philadelphia, PA: Templeton Foundation Press.

Teruya, S. (1996). *Relationship of beliefs and personality traits of misanthropy, anxiety, and sociability to prejudice*. Unpublished doctoral dissertation, Fuller Theological Seminary, Pasadena, CA.

Tonigan, J. S., Toscova, T. T., & Connors, G. J. (1999). Spirituality for the 12-step programs: A guide for clinicians. In W. R. Miller (Ed.), *Integrating spiri-*

tuality into treatment: Resources for practitioners (pp. 111–132). Washington, DC: American Psychological Association.

Triandis, H. C. (1971). *Attitude and attitude change*. Ann Arbor, MI: Books on Demand.

Turner, M. B. (1965). *Philosophy and the science of behavior*. New York: Appleton–Century–Crofts.

Vande Kemp, H. (1996). Psychology and Christian spirituality: Explorations of the inner world. *Journal of Psychology and Christianity, 15,* 161–174.

Vande Kemp, H. (1998). Christian psychologies for the twenty-first century: Lessons from history. *Journal of Psychology and Christianity, 17,* 197–209.

Vanden Burgt, R. J. (1981). *The religious philosophy of William James*. Chicago: Nelson-Hall.

Van Flanders, T. (1993). Dark matter, missing planets and new comets. Cited in J. D. Kooistra (1997), Paradigm shifty things. *Analog, 67* (6), 59–69.

Venable, G. D., & Gorsuch, R. L. (1999). I and E in developmental perspective. In L. Rector & W. Santaniello (Eds.), *Psychological perspectives and the religious quest* (pp. 81–101). New York: University Press of America.

Vitz, P. C. (1977). *Psychology as religion: The cult of self-worship*. Grand Rapids, MI: William B. Eerdmans.

Wade, S. H. (1989). *The development of a scale to measure forgiveness*. Unpublished doctoral dissertation, Fuller Theological Seminary, Pasadena, CA.

Wakeman, E. P., & Gorsuch, R. L. (1991). A test and expansion of the Fishbein model on religious attitudes and behavior in Thailand. *International Journal for the Psychology of Religion, 1,* 33–40.

Weaver, A. J., Samford, J. A., Kline, A. E., Lucas, L. A., Larson, D. B., & Koenig, H. G. (1997). What do psychologists know about working with the clergy? An analysis of eight APA journals: 1991–1994. *Professional Psychology: Research and Practice, 28,* 471–474.

Welhausen, J. (1957). *Prolegomena to the history of ancient Israel* (J. S. Black & A. Menzies, Trans.). Cleveland, OH: World Press.

Wong, A. (1999). *Beliefs, coping, control, and spiritual well-being: A multivariate model integrating psychology and Christianity*. Unpublished doctoral dissertation, Fuller Theological Seminary, Pasadena, CA.

Wong-McDonald, A., & Gorsuch, R. L. (1997). *Surrender to God: An additional coping style?* Unpublished master's thesis, Fuller Theological Seminary, Pasadena, CA.

Worthington, E. L. (Ed.). (1993). *Psychotherapy and religious values*. Grand Rapids, MI: Baker Books.

Wulff, D. M. (1997). *Psychology of religion: Classic and contemporary* (2d ed.). New York: Wiley.

Yahne, D. E., & Miller, W. R. (1999). Evoking hope. In W. R. Miller (Ed.), *Integrating spirituality into treatment: Resources for practitioners* (pp. 217–234). Washington, DC: American Psychological Association.

Zinnbauer, B. J., Pargament, K. I., Cole, B., Rye, M. S., Butter, E. M., Belavich, T. G., Hipp, K. M., Scott, A. B., & Kadar, J. L. (1997). Religion and spirituality: Unfuzzying the fuzzy. *Journal for the Scientific Study of Religion, 36,* 549–564.

Name Index

Subject Index

ABOUT THE AUTHOR

Richard L. Gorsuch is Professor of Psychology at Fuller Theological Seminary. Professor Gorsuch has published more than twenty books, manuals, or monographs and more than 120 papers in research methods, psychology of religion, and other areas of psychology.